INSTANT French

Vocabulary Builder

with Online Audio

Also by Tom Means:

Instant Spanish Vocabulary Builder with Online Audio

Inglés Instantáneo con Audio en Línea

Instant Italian Vocabulary Builder with Online Audio

INSTANT French
Vocabulary Builder
with Online Audio

TOM MEANS, PH.D.

HIPPOCRENE BOOKS, INC.
NEW YORK

Audio files available at

www.hippocrenebooks.com

Online audio edition, 2024.

Book design by Acme Klong Design.

For information, address:
HIPPOCRENE BOOKS, INC.
171 Madison Avenue
New York, NY 10016
www.hippocrenebooks.com

Previous edition
ISBN: 978-0-7818-0982-5

Cataloging-in-publication data available from the Library of Congress.

ISBN 978-0-7818-1448-5

CONTENTS

**excluding words ending in "–ical," which is a separate Chapter*

ACKNOWLEDGMENTS

I would like to give special thanks to Caitlin Davis, whose research helped make this book possible. Many thanks also to Marie-Cécile Vidican, whose translations of the stories and general consulting was invaluable. Thanks also to Jean-Christophe Henry and Bernadette Hoefer. Thanks to Gina Reid, Howard Means, and my parents, Tom and Anita, for incredible support. Thanks to my editor, Anne Kemper, for her steady and enthusiastic guidance, and also to my former editor, Caroline Gates.

I would like to express my gratitude to all the foreign language teachers who have clearly demonstrated many of these patterns in the past, especially Margarita Madrigal and Michel Thomas.

I dedicate this book to my son, Jude.

HOW WE LEARN LANGUAGES

Learning languages is at once a simple yet complex process. It's simple because in essence, we really only need to hear and see a language in order to learn it. If we hear and see a language often enough in contexts that are meaningful to us, we will eventually begin speaking and writing it.

It's complex because the human brain needs to see and hear the language for hundreds and hundreds of hours before it can start to make sense of its patterns and rules. If you can watch/read/listen to the new language enough times, then you can learn it. The ways in which you're exposed to a new language, however, must be meaningful to you in order to be memorable and impact your learning.

So it's complex but not impossible—just find speakers, books, videos, games, music, etc. in the new language and watch/play/read/listen to these resources every day. If the sources you use are memorable and meaningful to you and you have prolonged exposure to them, then after hundreds of hours spent with the new language, your brain will tell your mouth what to do, and abracadabra (!) you will be speaking this new language for the rest of your life.

There are only four ways to become exposed to a new language, so you don't have to worry about how to get started or how to continue toward your goal. The four modalities of language learning are READING, SPEAKING, LISTENING, and WRITING. This book and audio program provide some practice with all four modalities.

In order to learn a language, the first steps and most impactful modalities are LISTENING and READING. These allow learners to collect information (the other two modalities, speaking and writing, are aimed at producing the language once you get some "gas" in the tank). I strongly recommend watching television or movies in the new language. Here's the most important part: You will not understand everything you hear (sometimes it will feel like you don't understand anything!) but your brain will be making sense of all this valuable information so that it can eventually comprehend it and produce it. Try to find a TV program and dozens of movies that interest you in the new language. Watch them with a regular routine, even if it's only thirty minutes per day. And most importantly, keep watching and listening when you don't understand what they're saying! Your brain will make sense of it all but it needs the "nutrition" of hundreds of hours of input to make sense of it. Feed your brain the new language every day.

This book/online audio program provides obvious examples for listening and reading—read the words out loud in each chapter and listen to the examples and stories in each chapter. The reason I emphasize listening and reading first is because that's how we all learned our first language. Babies don't speak or write in their language until they've heard it and seen it for several years. This is very similar to what your brain needs for your new language. There are some differences between how a baby learns a first language and how children and adults learn second/third languages, but the fundamental requirement of hearing and seeing the language in abundance is the same for both.

The other two modalities are also important, you need to practice SPEAKING and WRITING in the new language in order to develop advanced levels of communication. This book/online audio program provides opportunities to practice writing and speaking—especially in the four exercises that end each of the chapters. You will be challenged to match words and to write simple sentences about the stories. For speaking, you should imitate the native speaker as he/she pronounces the words and expressions in every chapter (they are all set in **bold**), and you can also read the stories out loud to practice your pronunciation.

Lastly, I want to emphasize the importance of patience. Your brain can learn any language and it will do it very gradually. You only need to do four things, as summarized here:

- **Listen to/watch the language in material that interests you.** Keep watching even when you don't understand everything. After hundreds of hours of this, your brain will reward your efforts with understanding.

- **Read the language in material that interests you.** This can be anything that is written in the language: song lyrics, cartoons, illustrated books, magazines, websites, word games, etc. Keep reading because this will also help your ears eventually understand the listening task better.

- **Speak the language and make sure that what you are saying is important to you.** Practice speaking with a real person about your life, your family, your goals, your challenges. As you speak to someone, they will naturally respond and then you will also be working on your listening. Even if you can't find a conversation partner right now, imitate how people speak—when you are home, you can imitate people from videos and online speech.

- **Write the language and make sure you are writing about things that are authentic.** For example, try to write a description of your daily routine, your family, your residence, etc. If possible, find someone to provide you with some instruction. It does not have to be formal instruction but you will need some guidance.

For more information on these tips, please watch some videos on my YouTube channel, "Professor JT Means." If you have discipline, patience and interest in the new language (and you follow these steps) progress is inevitable.

INTRODUCTION

Instant French Vocabulary Builder can add thousands of words to your French vocabulary. It is designed to be a supplement for students of French at all levels. This book will help a student to learn to communicate effectively by dramatically increasing his/her French vocabulary.

There are thousands of English words that are connected to their French counterparts by word-ending patterns. This guide will illustrate those patterns and demonstrate how easily they work. The principal reason behind this is historical—the Norman Conquest. In the year 1066 the French conquered the British Isles and ruled there for many years, introducing thousands of French words into English. This means the two languages share thousands of closely related words, which makes vocabulary building much easier.

Vocabulary building is one of the keys for successful language learning. This book presents vocabulary patterns between English and French in such a systematic fashion that expanding your vocabulary will be easy and enjoyable. I believe it is the only one of its kind.

Instant French Vocabulary Builder is very easy to use. The 23 patterns presented in this book are based on word-endings (suffixes) and the chapters are listed alphabetically. For example, the first chapter presents English words that end in "–al" (*capital*, *normal*, etc.) Many of these words end in "–al" in French also (*capital*, *normal*, etc.)

The second chapter presents English words that end in "–ance" (distance, importance, etc.) Many of these words also end in "–ance" in French (*distance*, *importance*, etc.) In other cases, you only need to slightly change the ending of the English word to arrive at the correct French word. These words are commonly referred to as cognates: words related by common derivation or descent.

AUDIO ACCOMPANIMENT: This book comes with online audio accompaniment which is available for free download. Users can listen to the audio tracks online as well as download them to devices. Every chapter contains many recorded words that typify how words under that pattern are pronounced—all words **in bold** are on the recording. After each French word there will be a pause—it is *important* for the reader to imitate the native speaker during that pause.

Every chapter also contains common phrases and expressions that are recorded on the audio accompaniment. After every recorded expression there will be a pause for the reader to imitate the native speaker. All expressions **in bold** are on the recording.

In the exercise section of each chapter there are stories for the student to read and listen to with questions that follow. These stories are **in bold** and are also on the recording. They are read by a native speaker at standard speed. Students are not expected to understand every word of each story, but it is important for language learners to hear new vocabulary words used in an authentic context by a native speaker.

AUDIO FILES AVAILABLE AT:

EXERCISES: At the end of every chapter, there are exercises for the student to do. The first exercise is a matching exercise that reinforces the new words learned in the chapter. The second exercise is a story followed by questions. Every chapter contains a short story about Philippe and Marie, two young French people traveling through France.

ANSWER KEY: Answers for the exercises are available in the Answer Key section.

"FALSE FRIENDS": Sometimes the English word and the French word will look alike and sound alike, but have different meanings. These are often referred to as "false friends" or "false cognates." When this is the case, a more appropriate definition will be provided alongside the translation. One such example can be seen with the English word "library."

ENGLISH . . . . FRENCH
tutor . . . . tuteur *(meaning "guardian")*

In some rare cases, the English and French words possess such different meanings that the pair was not included in this book. For example, the meaning of the English word "appointment" has no relation to the meaning of the French word *appointements* (salary). In other rare cases, overly technical words were not included in this book.

DEVIATIONS IN SPELLING: Precise spelling of the French words may differ from the English words in more ways than just the endings. If you are interested in spelling the word correctly, please pay close attention to the French column. For example,

ENGLISH . . . . FRENCH
incredible . . . . incroyable

PRONUNCIATION GUIDE: *All bolded words in this brief pronunciation guide are recorded on the accompanying audio,* **Track 24**.

First, let's take a look at how French vowels are pronounced:

French vowel	Example	Approximate English sound
A	**parler**	ah
É	**téléphone**	hay
È	**très**	eh
I, Y	**merci**	ee
O	**Bordeaux**	oh
U	**université**	ooh

FRENCH NASAL COMBINATIONS

The following French nasal combinations and vowel combinations do not have English equivalents. Please listen to the accompanying CD to familiarize yourself with them:

Nasal combinations		French examples
an, am, **en**, em	=	***France, pense***
in, im, ain, **aim**, ein, yn, ym	=	***vin, faim***
on, om	=	***bonbon, ombre***

French vowel combinations		French examples
ou	=	***tour, cours***
ai, ei, ay, ey	=	***faire, meilleur***
oi, oy	=	***moi, voyage***
eu	=	***heure, peur***
au, eau	=	***chaud, beau***

There are a few pairings that produce distinct sounds that we will go over next.

The following combinations with the letter "c" and "ç" always produce a soft sound, as in "city": "ce," ***cerise*** (cherry); "ci," ***cité*** (city); "ça," ***façade*** (facade); "ço," ***glaçon*** (ice cube); "çu," ***déçu*** (disappointed)

The "j" produces a sound similar to the "s" in the English word "pleasure": ***jardin*** (garden)

The pairings "ge" and "gi" produce the same sound as above: ***plage*** (beach), ***magique*** (magical). The pairings "gea," "geo," and "geu" also produce the same sound: ***mangeant*** (eating), ***plongeon*** (dive), ***avantageux*** (advantageous)

A single "s" between two vowels sounds like the English "z" or "s" in "easy": ***maison*** (house), ***magasin*** (store)

The "ch" sounds like the "ss" in the English word "passion": ***charme*** (charm), ***chemise*** (shirt)

The "ill" sounds like the English word "eye": ***taille*** (size); ***maillot*** (bathing suit)

The "gn" is close to the "ny" in "canyon": ***gagner*** (to win); ***régner*** (to reign)

Lastly, the letter "h" is silent in French: ***hôtel*** (hotel), ***cathédrale*** (cathedral)

IMPORTANT NOTE ON GENDER: Unless otherwise noted in the chapter introduction, all French nouns and adjectives listed in this book are in the singular, masculine form. All nouns are listed without the article that typically accompanies them.

WORKS CONSULTED:

Dictionnaire Hachette Oxford, Français-Anglais Anglais-Français, Le dictionnaire bilingue interactif. New York: Oxford University Press; Paris: Hachette Multimedia, 1997.

Larouse French/English English/French Dictionary, Unabridged. Paris: Larousse, 1993.

Merriam-Webster's Collegiate Dictionary, Tenth Edition. Springfield, MA: Merriam-Webster, 2000.

Kirk-Greene, C. W. E. *NTC's Dictionary of Faux Amis*. Chicago: NTC Publishing Group, 1990.

Oates, Michael and Oukada, Larbi. *Entre Amis, 4th Edition*. Boston: Houghton-Mifflin Company, 2002.

Thody, Philip and Evans, Howard. *Mistakable French, Faux Amis and Key Words*. New York: Hippocrene Books, 1998.

Thomas, Michel. *French with Michel Thomas*. Chicago: NTC Publishing Group, 2000.

A NOTE FROM THE AUTHOR

When I first started studying French, I translated an old trick I had learned from Italian: Most English words that end in "–tion" stay the same in French. I was confident that my *communication* would be fine for any *situation* in which I would find myself. I was sure that everyone would have plenty of *admiration* for my mastery of French!

I know that this vocabulary bridge has aided my French skills greatly and fed my enthusiasm for learning and using a beautiful language.

In this book I have collected the 23 most common and applicable vocabulary bridges that exist between English and French. I have done this in the hope that readers find the same immediate application I did early in my language studies. I hope you find them useful.

A NOTE TO THE USER

The focus of this book is on vocabulary development. However, as with all effective language materials, the vocabulary has been set in an authentic cultural context with realistic characters and stories to encourage immediate applicability in real-life situations.

The exercises are suitable for individual and group work. Teachers will find that the 23 chapters easily can be incorporated into a one-year curriculum.

Chapter 1 

Many English words ending in "–al" have the same ending in French (excluding words ending in "–ical," which is a separate chapter).

French words ending in "–al" are usually adjectives. For example,

a <u>general</u> idea = *une idée <u>générale</u>*

All words and phrases in **bold** *are on* **Track 1** *of the accompanying audio.*

ENGLISH . . . . FRENCH

abdominal . . . . abdominal
abnormal . . . . anormal
admiral . . . . amiral
adverbial . . . . adverbial
amoral . . . . amoral
ancestral . . . . ancestral
animal . . . . **animal**
"It's an animal." . . . . **« C'est un animal. »**
anticolonial. . . . . anticolonial
antisocial . . . . antisocial
arsenal. . . . . arsenal
artisanal. . . . . artisanal
asocial . . . . asocial
astral . . . . astral
autumnal . . . . automnal
axial . . . . axial

banal. . . . . banal
baptismal . . . . baptismal
bestial . . . . bestial
bifocal . . . . bifocal

bilateral . . . . bilatéral
brutal. . . . . **brutal**
"It's a brutal reaction.". . . . . . **« C'est une réaction brutale. »**

canal . . . . canal *(also used for "TV channel")*
capital . . . . **capital** *(used for finance or "important"; for geography, use "capitale")*
cardinal . . . . cardinal
carnival . . . . carnaval *(also used for period of "Mardi Gras")*
causal . . . . causal
central . . . . **central**
cerebral . . . . cérébral
ceremonial . . . . cérémonial
collateral . . . . collatéral
colonial . . . . colonial
colossal . . . . colossal
commercial. . . . . commercial *(only an adjective)*
communal. . . . . communal
confessional . . . . confessionnal
conjugal. . . . . conjugal
continental . . . . **continental**
convivial. . . . . convivial
cordial . . . . cordial
corporal . . . . caporal
crucial . . . . **crucial**
"It's a crucial element." . . . . . **« C'est un élément crucial. »**

decimal . . . . décimal
departmental. . . . . départemental
diagonal. . . . . **diagonal**
dictatorial . . . . dictatorial
disloyal . . . . déloyal
doctoral . . . . doctoral
doctrinal. . . . . doctrinal
dorsal . . . . dorsal

ducal . . . . ducal

editorial . . . . éditorial
electoral . . . . èlectoral
Episcopal . . . . èpiscopal
equal . . . . **égal**
equatorial. . . . . équatorial
equilateral . . . . équilatéral
experimental. . . . . expérimental

facial . . . . facial
familial. . . . . familial
fatal. . . . . fatal *(also used for "inevitable")*
federal . . . . fédéral
fetal . . . . fœtal
feudal . . . . féodal
final. . . . . **final**
fiscal . . . . fiscal
floral . . . . floral
focal . . . . focal
frontal . . . . frontal
frugal. . . . . frugal
fundamental . . . . **fondamental**

gastrointestinal . . . . gastro-intestinal
general . . . . **général**
genial . . . . génial *(meaning "brilliant," "fantastic")*
genital . . . . génital
germinal. . . . . germinal
glacial . . . . glacial *(meaning "freezing cold")*
global . . . . global
guttural. . . . . guttural

hexagonal . . . . hexagonal
horizontal. . . . . horizontal
hormonal . . . . hormonal

hospital . . . . **hôpital**

ideal . . . . **idéal**
illegal. . . . . **illégal**
"Stealing is illegal.". . . . . **« Voler, c'est illégal. »**
immoral . . . . immoral
impartial. . . . . impartial
imperial . . . . impérial
inaugural . . . . inaugural
infernal . . . . infernal
infinitesimal . . . . infinitésimal
initial . . . . **initial**
instrumental . . . . instrumental *(only used in a musical context)*
integral . . . . intégral
intercontinental . . . . intercontinental
international . . . . **international**
"It's an international airport." . . . **« C'est un aéroport international. »**
intestinal. . . . . intestinal

journal . . . . journal *(also used for "newspaper")*
jovial . . . . jovial

lateral . . . . latéral
legal . . . . **légal**
lethal . . . . létal *(more commonly* "mortel" *or* "fatal"*)*
liberal . . . . libéral
literal . . . . littéral
local . . . . local *(also used for "commercial premises")*
longitudinal. . . . . longitudinal
loyal . . . . loyal

marginal. . . . . marginal
marital . . . . marital
marshal . . . . maréchal

marsupial . . . . marsupial
martial . . . . martial
matrimonial . . . . matrimonial
medical . . . . médical
medicinal . . . . médicinal
medieval . . . . médiéval
memorial . . . . mémorial *(only a noun)*
mental . . . . **mental**
meridional . . . . méridional *(meaning "Southern")*
metal . . . . métal
mineral. . . . . minéral
minimal . . . . minimal
monumental . . . . monumental
moral . . . . moral
multinational . . . . multinational *(also used for "international company")*
municipal . . . . municipal
mural . . . . mural
musical. . . . . musical

nasal . . . . nasal
natal . . . . natal
national . . . . **national**
naval . . . . naval
nominal . . . . nominal
normal . . . . normal
numeral . . . . numéral
nuptial . . . . nuptial

octagonal . . . . octogonal
occidental. . . . . occidental *(meaning "Western")*
optimal. . . . . optimal
oral . . . . oral
orbital . . . . orbital
orchestral . . . . orchestral
ordinal . . . . ordinal

oriental . . . . oriental *(meaning "Eastern")*
original . . . . **original**
"It's an original idea!" . . . . . . **« C'est une idée originale ! »**
ornamental . . . . ornemental

papal. . . . . papal
paradoxical . . . . paradoxal
paranormal. . . . . paranormal
parental . . . . parental
parochial . . . . paroissial
partial . . . . partial *(only used for "biased")*
pastoral . . . . pastoral
patriarchal . . . . patriarcal
pectoral . . . . pectoral
penal . . . . pénal
phenomenal . . . . phénoménal
pictorial . . . . pictural
postal. . . . . postal
postnatal . . . . postnatal
primal . . . . primal *(more commonly* "primitif"*)*
primordial . . . . primordial
principal. . . . . **principal**
professorial. . . . . professoral
proverbial. . . . . proverbial
provincial . . . . provincial

racial . . . . racial
radial. . . . . radial
radical . . . . radical
recital . . . . récital
rectal . . . . rectal
regional . . . . **régional**
rival . . . . rival
royal . . . . royal
rural. . . . . rural

sculptural . . . . sculptural
senatorial . . . . sénatorial
sentimental . . . . sentimental
sepulchral. . . . . sépulcral
signal. . . . . signal
social . . . . **social** *(more commonly* "sociable"*)*
spatial . . . . spatial
special . . . . **spécial**
"It's a very special day." . . . . **« C'est un jour très spécial. »**
spectral . . . . spectral
spiral . . . . spiral *(more commonly* "en spirale"*)*
structural. . . . . structural
subliminal. . . . . subliminal

terminal . . . . terminal
territorial . . . . territorial
testimonial . . . . testimonial *(only an adjective; as a noun, use* "témoignage"*)*
thermal. . . . . thermal *(only used for waters, springs)*
tonal . . . . tonal
total. . . . . **total**
transcendental. . . . . transcendantal
transcontinental . . . . transcontinental
tribal . . . . tribal
tribunal . . . . tribunal *(meaning "courthouse")*
triumphal . . . . triomphal
trivial . . . . trivial *(also used for "coarse," "vulgar")*
tropical. . . . . **tropical**
"It's a tropical island." . . . . . . **« C'est une île tropicale. »**

unequal . . . . inégal
unilateral . . . . unilatéral
urinal . . . . urinal

verbal . . . . verbal
vertebral. . . . . vertébral

vertical . . . . vertical
viral . . . . viral
virginal. . . . . virginal
visceral . . . . viscéral
vital . . . . vital
vocal . . . . vocal

Sometimes English words ending in "–al" will correspond to "–el" in French. Following are fifteen (15) of the most commonly used words that follow this pattern:

artificial . . . . artificiel
confidential. . . . . confidentiel
cultural. . . . . culturel
criminal . . . . criminel
emotional . . . . émotionnel
essential . . . . essentiel
formal . . . . formel
individual . . . . individuel *(adjective only)*
material . . . . matériel
natural . . . . naturel
official . . . . officiel
personal. . . . . personnel
residential. . . . . résidentiel
traditional. . . . . traditionnel
virtual . . . . virtuel

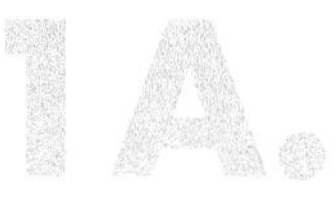

Match synonyms and/or associated words.
Reliez les paires de mots synonymes ou associés.

1. animal	convivial
2. total	unique
3. social	capital
4. original	complet
5. légal	essentiel
6. crucial	permis
7. principal	zoo

1B.

Listen to and read the story. Respond to the following questions in complete sentences.
Ecoutez et lisez l'histoire. Répondez aux questions suivantes avec des phrases complètes.

(This chapter presents the first story of the travels of Philippe and Marie. Every chapter will feature a new story about these two young French people traveling through France. Please listen to and read each story carefully before answering the questions that follow.)

Philippe et Marie sont deux jeunes de Strasbourg ; ils veulent partir en voyage (take a trip)**. Il y a un problème : Philippe veut faire un voyage international et Marie veut faire un voyage national. Philippe dit : « Mais Marie, ton idée n'est pas originale. » Marie dit : « Allons Philippe, pas maintenant** (not now)**! » Finalement, Marie gagne ; Philippe décide que ce n'est pas crucial de faire un voyage international maintenant. Marie a quelques idées générales pour leur itinéraire. Philippe dit :**

« Je ne veux pas rendre visite à ton oncle à Toulouse... il est trop antisocial et traditionnel ! » Marie dit : « On va voir... (we'll see)**. »**

1. D'où sont Philippe et Marie ?

2. Quel type de voyage veut faire Philippe ?

3. Quel type de voyage veut faire Marie ?

4. Que dit Philippe de l'idée de Marie ?

5. Selon Philippe (according to Philippe), comment est l'oncle de Marie ?

Chapter 2

Many English words ending "–ance" have the same ending in French.

French words ending in "–ance" are usually feminine nouns. For example,

arrogance = *l'arrogance*

All words and phrases in **bold** *are on* **Track 2** *of the accompanying audio.*

ENGLISH . . . . FRENCH

abundance . . . . abondance
alliance . . . . alliance *(also used for "marriage" or "wedding ring")*
ambiance . . . . ambiance
ambulance . . . . **ambulance**
"The patient is in the ambulance." . . . . **« Le patient est dans l'ambulance. »**
arrogance . . . . **arrogance**
assistance . . . . assistance
assonance . . . . assonance
assurance . . . . assurance *(also used for "insurance")*

balance . . . . balance *(more commonly "*équilibre*")*

chance . . . . chance
circumstance . . . . circonstance
clairvoyance . . . . clairvoyance
complaisance . . . . complaisance
concordance . . . . concordance
countenance . . . . contenance

defiance . . . . défiance *(meaning "distrust," "suspicion")*

deliverance. . . . . délivrance
dissonance . . . . dissonance
distance . . . . **distance**
dominance . . . . dominance

elegance. . . . . **élégance**
extravagance . . . . extravagance
exuberance. . . . . exubérance

finance. . . . . finance
flamboyance. . . . . flamboyance
fragrance . . . . fragrance

ignorance. . . . . ignorance
importance . . . . **importance**
insignificance . . . . insignifiance
intemperance . . . . intempérance
intolerance . . . . **intolérance**

lance . . . . lance

maintenance . . . . maintenance *(more commonly* "entretien"*)*

nonchalance . . . . nonchalance
nuance. . . . . nuance
nuisance. . . . . nuisance *(meaning "harmful effects")*

observance. . . . . observance *(only used in a religious context)*

performance . . . . performance
perseverance . . . . **persévérance**
"Perseverance is necessary." . . . **« Il faut de la persévérance. »**
predominance. . . . . prédominance
preponderance . . . . prépondérance
protuberance . . . . protubérance

reconnaissance . . . . reconnaissance
reluctance. . . . . réluctance
Renaissance . . . . Renaissance
resistance . . . . résistance
resonance. . . . . résonance
romance. . . . . romance *(meaning a genre of literature and music)*

séance . . . . séance *(meaning "session" or "meeting")*
substance . . . . **substance**
surveillance. . . . . surveillance

temperance. . . . . tempérance
tolerance . . . . **tolérance**
"Tolerance is a great quality." . . . . **« La tolérance est une grande qualité. »**

variance. . . . . variance
vengeance . . . . vengeance
vigilance . . . . vigilance

2A.

Reliez les paires de mots synonymes ou associés.

1. distance	proéminence
2. ambulance	respect
3. tolérance	hôpital
4. arrogance	parfum
5. importance	détermination
6. persévérance	loin
7. fragrance	vanité

2B.

Ecoutez et lisez l'histoire. Répondez aux questions suivantes avec des phrases complètes.

Pour organiser leur voyage, Philippe et Marie parlent de (discuss) **beaucoup de choses. Philippe parle de l'importance de ne pas dépenser beaucoup. Il sait qu'il y a beaucoup de distance à parcourir** (to cover) **et qu'il faudra** (it will be necessary to have) **de la persévérance. Marie elle aussi comprend l'importance de ne pas dépenser beaucoup d'argent. Elle demande une seule chose : elle veut voir un spectacle professionnel de danse en Corse. Philippe dit : « On va voir.... »**

1. Philippe parle de l'importance de quelle chose ?

2. Est-ce qu'il y a beaucoup de distance à parcourir ?

3. Qu'est-ce qu'il faudra ?

4. Est-ce que Marie comprend l'importance de ne pas dépenser beaucoup d'argent ?

5. Comment répond Philippe à la demande (request) de Marie ?

Chapter 3 

Many English words ending in "–ant" have the same ending in French.

French words ending in "–ant" can be nouns or adjectives. For example,

elegant (adj.) = *élégant*
a restaurant (n.) = *un restaurant*

All words and phrases in **bold** *are on* **Track 3** *of the accompanying audio.*

ENGLISH . . . . FRENCH

aberrant . . . . aberrant
abundant . . . . **abondant**
arrogant . . . . **arrogant**
ascendant . . . . ascendant
assailant . . . . assaillant
assistant . . . . assistant

brilliant . . . . brillant

chant . . . . chant *(meaning "melody" or "song")*
clairvoyant . . . . clairvoyant *(meaning "clear-sighted")*
colorant . . . . colorant
combatant . . . . combattant
commandant . . . . commandant
complaisant . . . . complaisant
concordant . . . . concordant
constant . . . . **constant** *(also used for "consistent")*
consultant . . . . consultant
croissant . . . . croissant
culminant . . . . culminant

defiant . . . . défiant *(meaning "suspicious")*

deodorant . . . . **déodorant**
descendant . . . . descendant
determinant . . . . déterminant
deviant . . . . déviant
discordant . . . . discordant
disinfectant . . . . désinfectant
dissonant . . . . dissonant
distant . . . . distant
dominant . . . . dominant
dormant . . . . dormant

elegant . . . . **élégant**
"He's an elegant man." . . . . . **« C'est un homme élégant. »**
elephant . . . . **éléphant**
emigrant . . . . émigrant
entrant . . . . entrant
errant . . . . errant
exorbitant . . . . exorbitant
expectorant . . . . expectorant
extravagant . . . . extravagant *(also used for "odd")*
exuberant . . . . exubérant

flagrant . . . . flagrant

gallant . . . . galant
giant . . . . géant

hesitant . . . . hésitant

ignorant . . . . **ignorant**
immigrant . . . . **immigrant**
important . . . . **important**
"It's an important detail." . . . . **« C'est un détail important. »**
incessant . . . . incessant
inconstant . . . . inconstant
infant . . . . enfant *(meaning "child")*

insignificant . . . . insignifiant
instant . . . . **instant**
intolerant . . . . intolérant
irritant . . . . irritant
itinerant . . . . itinérant

lieutenant . . . . lieutenant
lubricant. . . . . lubrifiant

migrant . . . . migrant
militant. . . . . militant
mutant . . . . mutant

nonchalant . . . . nonchalant

occupant . . . . **occupant**

participant . . . . **participant**
pedant . . . . pédant
penchant . . . . penchant
piquant . . . . piquant
pliant . . . . pliant
pleasant . . . . plaisant
poignant. . . . . poignant
predominant . . . . prédominant
preponderant . . . . prépondérant
Protestant . . . . Protestant *(lowercase if adjective)*

radiant. . . . . radiant
recalcitrant . . . . récalcitrant
redundant. . . . . redondant
refrigerant . . . . réfrigérant
relaxant . . . . relaxant
repentant . . . . repentant
repugnant. . . . . répugnant
resistant . . . . résistant
resonant. . . . . résonant

restaurant . . . . **restaurant**
resultant . . . . résultant

savant . . . . savant
servant . . . . servante
stagnant . . . . stagnant
stimulant . . . . **stimulant** *(also used for "stimulating")*
suppliant . . . . suppliant

tolerant . . . . tolérant
triumphant . . . . **triomphant**

vacant . . . . vacant *(more commonly "libre")*
vibrant . . . . vibrant
vigilant . . . . vigilant

Reliez les paires de mots synonymes ou associés.

1. restaurant	étranger
2. important	copieux
3. élégant	animal
4. abondant	essentiel
5. arrogant	chic
6. immigrant	dîner
7. éléphant	vanité

Ecoutez et lisez l'histoire. Répondez aux questions suivantes avec des phrases complètes.

Philippe et Marie décident de visiter d'abord une ville importante : Paris ! Marie dit : « Mais Philippe, c'est vrai que les gens (the people) **à Paris sont arrogants ? » Philippe répond : « Mais ne sois pas si ignorante ! Non, les Parisiens ne sont pas arrogants, leur façon de s'habiller** (way of dressing) **est très élégante et ils savent que l'histoire de Paris est très importante, mais... ce sont des gens très sympathiques. » Philippe a un ami, André, qui vit à Paris et a un restaurant qui s'appelle L'éléphant rouge. Dès qu'ils arrivent** (as soon as they arrive) **à Paris, ils vont manger au restaurant d'André. Il leur sert un dîner délicieux.**

1. Dans quelle ville vont Philippe et Marie ?

2. Que pense Marie des gens à Paris ?

3. Que dit Philippe de la façon de s'habiller des Parisiens ?

4. Comment Philippe décrit-il l'histoire de Paris ?

5. Comment s'appelle le restaurant d'André ?

Chapter 4

English words ending in "–ar" often correspond to "–aire" in French.

French words ending in "–aire" are usually nouns or adjectives. For example,

grammar (n.) = *la grammaire*
spectacular (adj.) = *spectaculaire*

All words and phrases in **bold** *are on* **Track 4** *of the accompanying audio.*

ENGLISH . . . . FRENCH

angular . . . . angulaire
antinuclear . . . . antinucléaire

binocular . . . . binoculaire
bipolar. . . . . bipolaire

cardiovascular . . . . cardio-vasculaire
cellular. . . . . **cellulaire** *(mostly used for "cellular phone" in Canada)*
circular. . . . . **circulaire**
consular . . . . consulaire

exemplar . . . . exemplaire

glandular . . . . glandulaire
globular . . . . globulaire
grammar . . . . grammaire

insular . . . . insulaire
intramuscular . . . . intramusculaire

jugular . . . . jugulaire

linear . . . . linéaire
lunar . . . . lunaire

modular . . . . modulaire
molar . . . . molaire *(only a noun)*
molecular . . . . moléculaire
muscular. . . . . musculaire *(meaning "of the muscle")*

nuclear. . . . . **nucléaire**
"It uses nuclear energy." . . . . **« Ça utilise l'énergie nucléaire. »**

peninsular. . . . . péninsulaire
perpendicular . . . . perpendiculaire
polar . . . . **polaire**
popular . . . . **populaire** *(also used for "of the common people")*

rectangular . . . . rectangulaire

secular . . . . séculaire
seminar . . . . séminaire *(also used for "seminary")*
solar . . . . solaire
spectacular . . . . **spectaculaire**
"It's a spectacular concert!" . . . **« C'est un concert spectaculaire ! »**
stellar. . . . . stellaire

thermonuclear . . . . thermonucléaire
tubular . . . . tubulaire

unpopular. . . . . impopulaire

vascular . . . . vasculaire
vulgar . . . . **vulgaire**

Reliez les paires de mots synonymes ou associés.

1. spectaculaire	soleil
2. polaire	indécent
3. solaire	cœur
4. circulaire	atomique
5. nucléaire	sphérique
6. vulgaire	froid
7. cardio-vasculaire	sensationnel

Ecoutez et lisez l'histoire. Répondez aux questions suivantes avec des phrases complètes.

Pendant qu'ils sont à Paris, Philippe et Marie font une promenade (go for a walk) **avec André. Pendant la promenade, le téléphone portable d'André sonne** (rings) **et il commence à parler italien. Son italien est spectaculaire. Marie est surprise qu'il parle si bien. Marie lui demande : « De quoi est-ce que tu parlais ? Ton italien est spectaculaire ! » André répond : « Merci, c'était mon ami qui étudie la physique nucléaire—j'adore parler italien avec lui, mais ses conversations sont plutôt** (quite) **circulaires, il ne parle que de la physique nucléaire ! » Marie dit : « Je suis très impressionnée, "Signor André," maintenant… où est-ce que nous allons ? »**

1. Que font-ils avec André ?

2. Quel type de téléphone est-ce qu'André utilise ?

3. Comment est l'italien d'André ?

4. Qu'est-ce que l'ami d'André étudie ?

5. Comment André décrit-il les conversations de son ami ?

Chapter 5

English words ending in "–ary" generally correspond to "–aire" in French.

French words ending in "–aire" are usually nouns or adjectives. For example,

a dictionary (n.) = *un dictionnaire*
extraordinary (adj.) = *extraordinaire*

All words and phrases in **bold** *are on* **Track 5** *of the accompanying audio.*

ENGLISH	FRENCH
adversary	adversaire
alimentary	alimentaire
anniversary	**anniversaire** *(also used for "birthday")*
apothecary	apothicaire
arbitrary	arbitraire
auxiliary	auxiliaire
beneficiary	bénéficiaire
bestiary	bestiaire
binary	binaire
breviary	bréviaire
budgetary	budgétaire
commentary	commentaire
commissary	commissaire
complementary	complémentaire
contrary	**contraire**
corollary	corollaire
coronary	coronaire
culinary	culinaire
depositary	dépositaire

dictionary . . . . **dictionnaire**
"He's using the dictionary." . . . **« Il utilise le dictionnaire. »**
dignitary . . . . dignitaire
disciplinary. . . . . disciplinaire
discretionary. . . . . discrétionnaire
documentary. . . . . documentaire

elementary . . . . élémentaire
emissary. . . . . émissaire
epistolary . . . . épistolaire
estuary. . . . . estuaire
exemplary . . . . exemplaire
extraordinary . . . . **extraordinaire**

fiduciary. . . . . fiduciaire
fragmentary . . . . fragmentaire
functionary . . . . fonctionnaire *(meaning "government employee")*

glossary . . . . **glossaire**

hereditary. . . . . héréditaire
honorary . . . . honoraire

imaginary . . . . **imaginaire**
incendiary . . . . incendiaire
intermediary . . . . intermédiaire
involuntary . . . . involontaire
itinerary . . . . **itinéraire**

judiciary. . . . . judiciaire

lapidary . . . . lapidaire
legendary. . . . . légendaire
literary . . . . littéraire

mercenary . . . . mercenaire
military. . . . . militaire
missionary . . . . missionnaire
monetary . . . . monétaire
mortuary . . . . mortuaire

necessary . . . . **nécessaire**
"It's not necessary." . . . . **« Ce n'est pas nécessaire. »**

ordinary . . . . **ordinaire**
ovary . . . . ovaire

parliamentary . . . . parlementaire
penitentiary . . . . pénitentiaire
preliminary. . . . . préliminaire
primary . . . . primaire
proprietary . . . . propriétaire *(meaning "owner")*
pulmonary . . . . pulmonaire

questionary. . . . . questionnaire *(meaning "questionnaire")*

reactionary. . . . . réactionnaire *(meaning "ultraconservative")*
revolutionary . . . . **révolutionnaire**
rosary . . . . rosaire
rudimentary . . . . rudimentaire

salary . . . . **salaire**
sanctuary . . . . sanctuaire
sanitary . . . . sanitaire
secondary . . . . secondaire
secretary . . . . **secrétaire**
sedentary . . . . sédentaire
sedimentary . . . . sédimentaire
seminary . . . . séminaire *(also used for "seminar")*
solitary. . . . . **solitaire**

stationary . . . . stationnaire
summary . . . . sommaire
supplementary. . . . . supplémentaire

temporary. . . . . temporaire
tertiary . . . . tertiaire
tributary . . . . tributaire *(only used for "paying tribute")*

unitary . . . . unitaire
urinary . . . . urinaire

veterinary. . . . . vétérinaire
visionary . . . . visionnaire
vocabulary . . . . **vocabulaire**
"I learn the vocabulary." . . . . **« J'apprends le vocabulaire. »**
voluntary . . . . volontaire *(also used for "volunteer")*

5A.

Reliez les paires de mots synonymes ou associés.

1. nécessaire	définition
2. ordinaire	obligatoire
3. contraire	argent
4. anniversaire	assistant
5. dictionnaire	commun
6. salaire	opposé
7. secrétaire	célébration

5B.

Ecoutez et lisez l'histoire. Répondez aux questions suivantes avec des phrases complètes.

Philippe et Marie ont un itinéraire très compliqué à Paris. Pour ne pas oublier (in order to not forget) **leurs aventures, Marie veut louer** (to rent) **un caméscope pour filmer un documentaire. Un jour ils vont au Louvre, un autre jour à Notre-Dame, et un autre jour ils vont à Montmartre. Philippe dit : « Ce rythme est extraordinaire ! » Chaque jour, Marie filme son documentaire, mais Philippe ne comprend pas. Il dit : « Ce n'est pas nécessaire de filmer chaque détail** (every detail)**. » Marie répond : « Au contraire, c'est très important de filmer chaque détail ! »**

1. Comment est l'itinéraire de Philippe et Marie à Paris ?

2. Qu'est-ce que Marie filme avec son caméscope ?

3. Que dit Philippe du rythme ?

4. Selon Philippe, il n'est pas nécessaire de faire quoi ?

5. Que répond Marie ?

Chapter 6

Many English words ending in "–ble" have the same ending in French.

French words ending in "–ble" are usually adjectives. For example,

a <u>horrible</u> film = *un film <u>horrible</u>*

All words and phrases in **bold** *are on* **Track 6** *of the accompanying audio.*

ENGLISH . . . . FRENCH

abominable . . . . abominable
absorbable . . . . absorbable
acceptable . . . . **acceptable**
accessible. . . . . accessible
adaptable. . . . . adaptable
adjustable. . . . . ajustable
admirable. . . . . admirable
admissible . . . . admissible
adorable . . . . **adorable**
"This child is adorable." . . . . **« Cet enfant est adorable. »**
affable . . . . affable
agreeable. . . . . agréable
amiable . . . . amiable *(meaning "friendly terms")*
applicable . . . . applicable
appreciable . . . . appréciable
arable . . . . arable
audible . . . . audible

Bible . . . . Bible
biodegradable . . . . biodégradable

cable . . . . câble
calculable. . . . . calculable

capable . . . . capable
charitable. . . . . charitable
combustible . . . . combustible
comfortable . . . . confortable *(only used for objects, not people)*
communicable. . . . . communicable
comparable . . . . **comparable**
compatible . . . . compatible
comprehensible. . . . . compréhensible
condemnable . . . . condamnable
considerable. . . . . considérable
constructible . . . . constructible
contestable . . . . contestable
controllable. . . . . contrôlable
corrigible . . . . corrigible
credible . . . . **crédible**
cultivable . . . . cultivable
curable. . . . . curable

deductible . . . . déductible *(more commonly "*franchise*" as a noun)*
defendable . . . . défendable
delectable. . . . . délectable
demonstrable . . . . démontrable
deplorable . . . . déplorable
desirable . . . . désirable
destructible . . . . destructible
detachable . . . . détachable
detectable. . . . . détectable
determinable. . . . . déterminable
detestable. . . . . détestable
digestible . . . . digestible *(more commonly "*digeste*")*
dirigible . . . . dirigeable
disagreeable. . . . . désagréable
discernable. . . . . discernable
disposable . . . . disponible *(meaning "available")*

divisible . . . . **divisible**
double . . . . double
durable . . . . durable

eligible. . . . . éligible
employable. . . . . employable
ensemble . . . . ensemble
enviable . . . . enviable
equitable . . . . équitable
estimable . . . . estimable
evitable . . . . évitable
excitable . . . . excitable
excusable . . . . **excusable**
"The mistake is excusable." . . **« L'erreur est excusable. »**
explicable. . . . . explicable
exploitable . . . . exploitable
exportable . . . . exportable
extensible . . . . extensible

fable . . . . fable
fallible . . . . faillible
favorable . . . . favorable
feasible . . . . faisable
feeble . . . . faible
flexible. . . . . **flexible**
formidable . . . . formidable *(meaning "great!" or "super!")*

governable . . . . gouvernable

habitable . . . . habitable
honorable. . . . . honorable
horrible . . . . **horrible**
"It's a horrible accident." . . . . **« C'est un accident horrible. »**
humble. . . . . humble

identifiable	identifiable
ignoble	ignoble
imaginable	imaginable
imitable	imitable
impassible	impassible
impeccable	**impeccable**
impenetrable	impénétrable
imperceptible	imperceptible
impermeable	imperméable *(also used for "raincoat")*
imperturbable	imperturbable
implacable	implacable
impossible	**impossible**
"That's impossible!"	**« C'est impossible ! »**
impressionable	impressionnable
improbable	**improbable**
inaccessible	inaccessible
inadmissible	inadmissible
inalienable	inaliénable
inalterable	inaltérable
inapplicable	inapplicable
inappreciable	inappréciable *(meaning "priceless")*
inaudible	inaudible
incalculable	incalculable
incapable	incapable
incompatible	incompatible
incomprehensible	incompréhensible
inconsolable	inconsolable
incontestable	incontestable
incorrigible	incorrigible
incredible	**incroyable**
incurable	incurable
indefensible	indéfendable
indefinable	indéfinissable
indelible	indélébile
indescribable	indescriptible
indestructible	indestructible

indispensable . . . . indispensable
indivisible. . . . . indivisible
indubitable . . . . indubitable
ineffable. . . . . ineffable
inestimable . . . . inestimable
inevitable . . . . **inévitable**
inexcusable . . . . inexcusable
inexorable . . . . inexorable
inexplicable . . . . inexplicable
infallible . . . . infaillible
inflammable . . . . inflammable
inflexible . . . . **inflexible**
inhabitable . . . . habitable
inimitable . . . . inimitable
innumerable . . . . innombrable
inoperable . . . . inopérable
insatiable . . . . insatiable
insensible . . . . insensible *(meaning "insensitive")*
inseparable . . . . inséparable
insoluble. . . . . insoluble
intangible . . . . intangible
intelligible. . . . . intelligible
interminable . . . . interminable
intolerable . . . . intolérable
invariable. . . . . invariable
invincible . . . . invincible
inviolable . . . . inviolable
invisible . . . . **invisible**
invulnerable . . . . invulnérable
irascible . . . . irascible
irreconcilable . . . . irréconciliable
irreducible . . . . irréductible
irrefutable. . . . . irréfutable
irreparable . . . . irréparable
irrepressible . . . . irrépressible
irresistible. . . . . irrésistible

irresponsible . . . . **irresponsable**
irreversible . . . . irréversible
irrevocable . . . . irrévocable
irrigable . . . . irrigable
irritable . . . . irritable

justifiable . . . . justifiable

lamentable . . . . lamentable *(also used for "pitiful," "pathetic")*
legible . . . . lisible
limitable . . . . limitable

malleable . . . . malléable
maneuverable . . . . manœuvrable
measurable. . . . . mesurable
memorable . . . . mémorable
miserable . . . . **misérable**
modifiable . . . . modifiable

navigable . . . . navigable
negligible . . . . négligeable
negotiable . . . . négociable
noble . . . . **noble**
notable. . . . . notable

observable . . . . observable
operable . . . . opérable
opposable . . . . opposable
ostensible . . . . ostensible

palpable. . . . . palpable
pardonable. . . . . pardonnable
passable. . . . . **passable**
payable . . . . payable
penetrable . . . . pénétrable

perceptible . . . . perceptible
permeable . . . . perméable
pitiable. . . . . pitoyable
plausible . . . . plausible
pliable . . . . pliable
portable . . . . portable *(also used for "wearable" and "cell phone")*
possible . . . . **possible**
preferable. . . . . préférable
presentable. . . . . présentable
probable . . . . **probable**
profitable . . . . rentable
programmable . . . . programmable
provable. . . . . prouvable
punishable . . . . punissable

quantifiable . . . . quantifiable

realizable. . . . . réalisable
reasonable . . . . raisonnable
recognizable. . . . . reconnaissable
recommendable . . . . recommandable
recyclable. . . . . recyclable
reducible . . . . réductible
refutable. . . . . réfutable
remarkable . . . . remarquable
renewable . . . . renouvelable
repairable . . . . **réparable**
reprehensible . . . . répréhensible
respectable . . . . **respectable**
responsible . . . . **responsable**
retractable . . . . rétractable
reusable . . . . réutilisable
reversible . . . . réversible
revisable . . . . révisable
revocable . . . . révocable

sensible . . . . sensible *(meaning "sensitive")*
separable . . . . séparable
sociable . . . . sociable
stable . . . . **stable** *(only an adjective; "horse stable" is "écurie")*
supportable . . . . supportable
susceptible . . . . susceptible

table . . . . table
tangible . . . . tangible
terrible . . . . terrible *(also used for "great")*
tolerable . . . . tolérable
transferable . . . . transférable
transformable . . . . transformable
transportable . . . . transportable
traversable . . . . traversable
trouble . . . . trouble *(meaning "troublesome")*

unalterable . . . . inaltérable
uncontrollable . . . . incontrôlable
undesirable . . . . indésirable
unimaginable . . . . inimaginable
uninhabitable . . . . inhabitable
unrealizable . . . . irréalisable
unstable . . . . instable
untouchable . . . . intouchable
utilizable . . . . utilisable

variable . . . . **variable**
venerable . . . . vénérable
verifiable . . . . vérifiable
veritable . . . . véritable
viable . . . . viable
visible . . . . **visible**
vulnerable . . . . vulnérable

Reliez les paires de mots synonymes ou associés.

1. visible	extraordinaire
2. incroyable	rigide
3. horrible	mignon
4. inflexible	très mal
5. comparable	perceptible
6. probable	similaire
7. adorable	possible

Ecoutez et lisez l'histoire. Répondez aux questions suivantes avec des phrases complètes.

Après quelques jours à Paris, Philippe et Marie prennent l'avion pour la Corse. Pendant le voyage en avion ils se disputent (have an argument)**. Marie dit à Philippe : « Tu es très irresponsable ! Tu n'as pas reservé les places pour la danse ! » Philippe répond : « Tu es inflexible, nous pouvons y aller une autre fois** (another time) **; il est très probable que nous revenions en Corse un jour. » Marie dit : « Tu es impossible ! Il est assez improbable que nous retournions en Corse ! » Finalement, Philippe s'excuse** (apologizes) **et dit qu'il sera beaucoup plus responsable pendant le reste du voyage. Marie demande s'il sera possible d'acheter les billets pour le spectacle de danse en Corse. Philippe répond : « On va voir.... »**

1. Où est-ce qu'il vont après Paris ?

2. Que pense Marie de Philippe ?

3. Que dit Philippe de Marie ?

4. Est-ce que Marie pense qu'il est probable qu'ils retournent en Corse un jour ?

5. Que demande Marie à la fin ?

Chapter 7 

Many English words ending in "–ct" have the same ending in French.

French words ending in "–ct" can be adjectives or nouns. For example,

direct (adj.) = *direct*
a contact (n.) = *un contact*

All words and phrases in **bold** *are on* **Track 7** *of the accompanying audio.*

ENGLISH . . . . FRENCH

aspect . . . . **aspect**

circumspect. . . . . circonspect
compact. . . . . compact
contact . . . . **contact**
"I have a good contact." . . . . **« J'ai un bon contact. »**
correct . . . . **correct**

direct . . . . **direct**
"The train is direct." . . . . **« Le train est direct. »**
distinct . . . . distinct
district . . . . district

exact . . . . exact

impact . . . . impact
incorrect. . . . . **incorrect**
"That's incorrect." . . . . **« C'est incorrect. »**
indirect. . . . . **indirect**
indistinct. . . . . indistinct
inexact. . . . . inexact

instinct . . . . instinct
intact . . . . intact
intellect. . . . . intellect

respect . . . . **respect**

select . . . . sélect *(only an adjective)*
strict. . . . . strict
suspect. . . . . suspect

tact . . . . tact
tract. . . . . tract

verdict . . . . verdict

Reliez les paires de mots synonymes ou associés.

1. respect	précis
2. direct	adresse
3. correct	erroné
4. contact	immédiat
5. aspect	partie
6. exact	admiration
7. incorrect	exact

7B.

Ecoutez et lisez l'histoire. Répondez aux questions suivantes avec des phrases complètes.

Après le vol direct de Paris à Ajaccio, en Corse, Marie demande si leur destination est correcte parce qu'elle ne comprend pas tout (doesn't understand everything)**. Elle sait que le français parlé** (spoken French) **n'est pas toujours clair, mais elle ne comprend pas très bien ce dialecte ! Philippe dit : « Ne t'inquiète pas, j'ai un bon contact ici à Ajaccio, il s'appelle Alphonse, son français est excellent. » Après quelques minutes dans l'aéroport, Alphonse vient les chercher** (pick them up)**. Alphonse est très sympa et a beaucoup de respect pour son ami Philippe et sa petite amie Marie. Après un bon dîner chez Alphonse, Marie lui demande s'il sait quelque chose au sujet du spectacle dans le centre. Alphonse répond : « On va voir.... »**

1. Quel type de vol est-ce qu'ils ont pris (did they take) de Paris ?

2. Pourquoi est-ce que Marie pense que ce n'est pas la destination correcte ?

3. Pourquoi est-ce que Marie ne comprend pas le français en Corse ?

4. Comment s'appelle le contact de Philippe à Ajaccio ?

5. Que pense Alphonse de Philippe et de sa petite amie Marie ?

Chapter 8

Many English words ending in "–ence" have the same ending in French.

French words ending in "–ence" are usually feminine nouns. For example,

a coincidence = *une coïncidence*

All words and phrases in **bold** *are on* **Track 8** *of the accompanying audio.*

ENGLISH . . . . FRENCH

absence . . . . **absence**
abstinence . . . . abstinence
adherence . . . . adhérence
adolescence . . . . adolescence
ambivalence . . . . ambivalence
audience . . . . audience *(more commonly "*public*")*

cadence . . . . cadence
coexistence. . . . . coexistence
coherence. . . . . cohérence
coincidence. . . . . **coïncidence**
"It's a coincidence." . . . . **« C'est une coïncidence. »**
competence . . . . compétence
concurrence . . . . concurrence *(meaning "competition")*
conference . . . . **conférence**
confidence . . . . confidence *(meaning "secret/private information")*
conscience . . . . conscience
consequence . . . . **conséquence**
convalescence. . . . . convalescence
convergence . . . . convergence

decadence . . . . décadence
deference . . . . déférence
difference . . . . **différence**
divergence . . . . divergence

effervescence . . . . effervescence
eloquence. . . . . éloquence
emergence . . . . émergence
eminence . . . . éminence
equivalence . . . . équivalence
essence . . . . essence
evidence . . . . évidence *(meaning "obvious")*
excellence . . . . excellence
existence . . . . existence
experience . . . . **expérience** *(also used for "experiment")*
"He has no experience." . . . . **« Il n'a pas d'expérience. »**

flatulence . . . . flatulence

imminence . . . . imminence
impatience . . . . **impatience**
impertinence . . . . impertinence
impotence. . . . . impotence
impudence . . . . impudence
imprudence. . . . . imprudence
incandescence . . . . incandescence
incidence . . . . incidence *(also used for "impact")*
incoherence . . . . incohérence
incompetence . . . . incompétence
inconsequence . . . . inconséquence
incontinence . . . . incontinence
indifference. . . . . **indifférence**
indolence . . . . indolence
indulgence . . . . indulgence
inexperience . . . . inexpérience
influence. . . . . **influence**

innocence . . . . **innocence**
insolence . . . . insolence
intelligence . . . . **intelligence**
interference. . . . . interférence
irreverence . . . . irrévérence

jurisprudence . . . . jurisprudence

luminescence . . . . luminescence

magnificence . . . . magnificence
munificence . . . . munificence

negligence . . . . négligence

occurrence . . . . occurrence *(meaning "circumstances")*
omnipotence. . . . . omnipotence
omnipresence . . . . omniprésence
opulence . . . . opulence

patience . . . . **patience**
penitence . . . . pénitence
permanence . . . . permanence
pertinence . . . . pertinence
pestilence. . . . . pestilence
preeminence. . . . . prééminence
preference . . . . **préférence**
prescience . . . . prescience
presence. . . . . **présence**
prevalence . . . . prévalence
providence . . . . providence
prudence . . . . prudence

quintessence . . . . quintessence

recurrence . . . . récurrence

reference . . . . référence
reminiscence. . . . . réminiscence
residence . . . . **résidence**
reticence . . . . réticence
reverence . . . . révérence

science . . . . **science**
"I love science." . . . . **« J'aime la science. »**
sentence . . . . sentence *(meaning "prison sentence")*
sequence . . . . **séquence**
silence . . . . silence

transparence. . . . . transparence
truculence . . . . truculence
turbulence. . . . . turbulence

vehemence . . . . véhémence
videoconference . . . . vidéoconférence
violence . . . . **violence**
virulence. . . . . virulence

Reliez les paires de mots synonymes ou associés.

1. patience	naïveté
2. différence	calme
3. innocence	distinction
4. violence	maturité
5. science	réunion
6. conférence	biologie
7. expérience	guerre

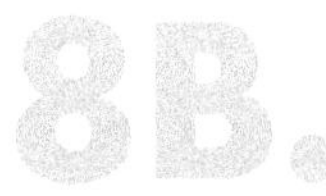

Ecoutez et lisez l'histoire. Répondez aux questions suivantes avec des phrases complètes.

Le jour suivant, Alphonse dit à Marie : « Quelle coïncidence ! Ma petite amie et moi, nous allons à la danse demain soir, vous voulez venir avec nous ? » Le lendemain (the next day), **Marie est très contente et dit à Philippe : « Tu vois ? La persistance et la patience aident. » Philippe est très content que Marie soit heureuse** (that she's happy) **et pense que ça sera une bonne expérience. Malheureusement Philippe n'a pas beaucoup de patience ni d'intérêt pour la danse. Il essaie de cacher** (he tries to hide) **son indifférence. Philippe dit à Marie : « Je suis désolé pour mon impatience, mais... la danse est horrible ! » Après deux jours avec Alphonse à Ajaccio, Philippe et Marie vont à Monaco.**

1. Que dit Alphonse de la danse ?

2. Selon Marie, quelles choses aident ?

3. A quoi s'attend Philippe (what does he expect) avant la danse ?

4. Est-ce que Philippe ressent (feels) de la passion ou de l'indifférence pour la danse ?

5. Pourquoi Philippe s'excuse-t-il ?

Chapter 9

English words ending in "–ent" often have the same ending in French.

French words ending in "–ent" can be adjectives or nouns. For example,

different (adj.) = *différent*
an ingredient (n.) = *un ingrédient*

All words and phrases in **bold** *are on* **Track 9** *of the accompanying audio.*

ENGLISH . . . . FRENCH

abasement . . . . abaissement
absent . . . . absent
accent . . . . accent
accident . . . . accident
accompaniment. . . . . accompagnement
adherent. . . . . adhérent
adjacent. . . . . adjacent
adjournment . . . . ajournement
adjustment . . . . reajustement
adolescent . . . . adolescent
adornment . . . . ornement
advancement . . . . avancement
advertisement . . . . avertissement *(meaning "warning")*
agent . . . . **agent**
agreement . . . . agrément
alignment . . . . alignement
ambivalent . . . . ambivalent
amendment. . . . . amendement
amusement . . . . amusement
antecedent . . . . antécédent
apartment. . . . . appartement
apparent . . . . apparent

appeasement . . . . apaisement
ardent . . . . ardent
argument . . . . argument *(meaning "deciding factor/point")*
armament . . . . armement
arrangement . . . . arrangement
assortment . . . . assortiment
astonishment . . . . étonnement
astringent . . . . astringent
attachment . . . . attachement *(only used for feelings)*

banishment . . . . bannissement
basement . . . . soubassement
bombardment . . . . bombardement

cement . . . . ciment
chastisement . . . . châtiment
client . . . . **client**
coefficient . . . . coefficient
coherent . . . . cohérent
coincident . . . . coïncident
commandment . . . . commandement
commencement . . . . commencement
compartment . . . . compartiment
competent . . . . **compétent**
"The teacher is competent." . . . **« Le professeur est compétent. »**
complement . . . . complément
compliment . . . . compliment
comportment . . . . comportement
condiment . . . . condiment
confident . . . . confident *(meaning "confidant")*
consent . . . . consentement
consequent . . . . conséquent
content . . . . content
contentment . . . . contentement
continent . . . . **continent**

contingent	contingent
convalescent	convalescent
convent	couvent
convergent	convergent
corpulent	corpulent
counterargument	contre-argument
decadent	décadent
decent	décent
deficient	déficient
department	département
deployment	déploiement
derailment	déraillement
derangement	dérangement
detachment	détachement
detergent	détergent
detriment	détriment
development	développement
different	**différent**
disagreement	désagrément *(meaning "annoyance")*
discernment	discernement
discontent	mécontentement
discouragement	découragement
dismemberment	démembrement
displacement	déplacement
dissident	dissident
divergent	divergent
document	document
effervescent	effervescent
element	élément
eloquent	éloquent
embarkment	embarquement
emergent	émergent
eminent	éminent
enchantment	enchantement

encouragement . . . . encouragement
endorsement . . . . endossement
engagement . . . . engagement *(only used for "arrangement"; for marriage, use "fiançailles")*
enlargement . . . . élargissement
enlightenment . . . . éclaircissement
enrichment . . . . enrichissement
enrollment. . . . . enrôlement
environment . . . . environnement
equipment . . . . équipement
equivalent. . . . . équivalent
establishment . . . . établissement
evanescent . . . . évanescent
event . . . . événement
evident. . . . . évident
excellent. . . . . excellent
excrement. . . . . excrément
expedient . . . . expédient

ferment. . . . . ferment *(only a noun)*
fervent . . . . fervent
filament . . . . filament
firmament . . . . firmament
fluorescent . . . . fluorescent
fragment. . . . . fragment
frequent . . . . **fréquent**

government. . . . . gouvernement
grandparent(s) . . . . grands-parents *(only used in the plural)*

harassment . . . . harcèlement

imminent . . . . imminent
impatient . . . . **impatient**
impertinent . . . . impertinent

impotent . . . . impotent
impoverishment . . . . appauvrissement
imprisonment . . . . emprisonnement
imprudent . . . . imprudent
impudent . . . . impudent
incandescent . . . . incandescent
incident . . . . incident
inclement . . . . inclément
incoherent . . . . incohérent
incompetent . . . . incompétent
inconsequent . . . . inconséquent
incontinent . . . . incontinent
inconvenient . . . . inconvénient *(only used as a noun, "inconvenience")*
indecent . . . . indécent
indifferent . . . . **indifférent**
"He's indifferent." . . . . **« Il est indifférent. »**
indigent . . . . indigent
indolent . . . . indolent
indulgent . . . . indulgent
ingredient . . . . **ingrédient**
inherent . . . . inhérent
innocent . . . . **innocent**
insolent . . . . insolent
instrument . . . . instrument
intelligent . . . . **intelligent**
intermittent . . . . intermittent
internment . . . . internement
investment . . . . investissement
irreverent . . . . irrévérent *(more commonly "irrespectueux")*

judgment . . . . jugement

latent . . . . latent
ligament . . . . ligament

moment . . . . moment
monument. . . . . monument
movement. . . . . mouvement
munificent. . . . . munificent

negligent . . . . négligent

omnipotent . . . . omnipotent
omnipresent . . . . omniprésent
omniscient . . . . omniscient
opulent. . . . . opulent
orient . . . . orient
ornament . . . . ornement

parent . . . . parent *(also used for "relative")*
parliament . . . . parlement
patient . . . . **patient**
"You're not very patient.". . . . **« Tu n'es pas très patient. »**
pavement . . . . pavement *(more commonly* "trottoir"*)*
payment. . . . . paiement
penitent . . . . pénitent
percent. . . . . pour cent
permanent . . . . **permanent**
pertinent. . . . . pertinent
phosphorescent . . . . phosphorescent
pigment . . . . pigment
placement. . . . . placement
precedent . . . . précédent
preeminent . . . . prééminent
prescient. . . . . prescient
present. . . . . **présent**
president . . . . **président**
"Here's the new president.". . . **« Voici le nouveau président. »**
prominent. . . . . proéminent *(only used for physical features)*
prudent . . . . prudent

quotient . . . . quotient

realignment. . . . . réalignement
recent. . . . . récent
recipient. . . . . récipient *(meaning "container")*
recruitment . . . . recrutement
re-establishment. . . . . rétablissement
refinement . . . . raffinement
refreshment. . . . . rafraîchissement
regiment. . . . . régiment
reimbursement. . . . . remboursement
reinforcement . . . . renforcement
reinvestment . . . . réinvestissement
replacement . . . . remplacement
resentment . . . . ressentiment
resident . . . . **résident**
reticent. . . . . réticent

sacrament. . . . . sacrement
sediment. . . . . sédiment
segment . . . . segment
sentiment . . . . sentiment
serpent. . . . . serpent
strident. . . . . strident
subcontinent . . . . sous-continent
succulent . . . . succulent
sufficient. . . . . suffisamment *(meaning "sufficiently," "enough")*
supplement . . . . supplément

talent . . . . talent
tangent . . . . **tangent**
temperament. . . . . tempérament
testament . . . . testament
torment. . . . . tourment
torrent . . . . torrent

transparent . . . . transparent
treatment . . . . traitement *(also used for "salary")*
trident . . . . trident
truculent . . . . truculent
turbulent . . . . turbulent

urgent . . . . **urgent**
"It's an urgent letter." . . . . **« C'est une lettre urgente. »**

vehement . . . . véhément
vice president . . . . vice-président
violent . . . . violent
virulent . . . . virulent

Reliez les paires de mots synonymes ou associés.

1. président	calme
2. urgent	intellectuel
3. continent	distinct
4. client	directeur
5. patient	consommateur
6. intelligent	pressant
7. différent	Europe

Ecoutez et lisez l'histoire. Répondez aux questions suivantes avec des phrases complètes.

Quand ils arrivent à Monaco, Marie appelle sa mère (calls her mother) **et reçoit un message urgent : elle doit rendre visite à son cousin à Monaco. Son cousin Nicolas est directeur d'un établissement médical. Philippe demande : « Décris ton cousin, comment est-il ? » Marie répond : « Eh bien, mon cousin est... différent... c'est un docteur très compétent et très, très intelligent, mais il est un peu étrange** (strange)**. » Philippe veut savoir pourquoi il est si « différent. » Marie lui dit : « Tu verras** (you'll see)**, il pense que nous sommes tous docteurs." Philippe dit : « Bon, on va voir.... »**

1. Quel type de message reçoit Marie ?

2. Nicolas est directeur de quoi ?

3. Que dit Marie de son cousin ?

4. Selon Marie, est-ce que Nicolas est intelligent ?

5. Que dit Philippe à la fin ?

Chapter 10

English words ending in "–gy" generally correspond to "–gie" in French.

French words ending in "–gie" are usually feminine nouns. For example,

a strategy = *une stratégie*

All words and phrases in **bold** *are on* **Track 10** *of the accompanying audio.*

ENGLISH . . . . FRENCH

allergy . . . . **allergie**
"I have a lot of allergies." . . . **« J'ai beaucoup d'allergies. »**
analogy . . . . analogie
anesthesiology . . . . anesthésiologie
anthology . . . . anthologie
anthropology . . . . anthropologie
archaeology . . . . archéologie
astrology . . . . astrologie

biology . . . . **biologie**
biotechnology . . . . biotechnologie

cardiology . . . . cardiologie
chronology . . . . **chronologie**
climatology . . . . climatologie
cosmology . . . . cosmologie
criminology . . . . criminologie

dermatology . . . . dermatologie

ecology . . . . écologie
effigy . . . . effigie

elegy . . . . élégie
endocrinology. . . . . endocrinologie
energy . . . . **énergie**
ethnology . . . . ethnologie
etymology. . . . . étymologie

gastroenterology . . . . gastro-entérologie
genealogy . . . . généalogie
geology . . . . **géologie**

ideology. . . . . **idéologie**

lethargy . . . . léthargie
liturgy . . . . liturgie

metallurgy . . . . métallurgie
meteorology . . . . **météorologie**
methodology. . . . . méthodologie
microbiology. . . . . microbiologie
mineralogy . . . . minéralogie
morphology . . . . morphologie
musicology . . . . musicologie
mythology . . . . **mythologie**
"I'm interested in mythology." . . **« Je m'intéresse à la mythologie. »**

neurology. . . . . neurologie

oncology . . . . oncologie
ontology. . . . . ontologie
orgy. orgie

paleontology. . . . . paléontologie
pathology. . . . . pathologie
pedagogy. . . . . pédagogie
philology . . . . philologie
phonology . . . . phonologie

phraseology . . . . phraséologie
physiology . . . . physiologie
psychology . . . . **psychologie**

radiology . . . . **radiologie**
rheumatology . . . . rhumatologie

seismology . . . . sismologie
sexology. . . . . sexologie
sociology . . . . sociologie
strategy . . . . **stratégie**
"It's an interesting strategy." . . **« C'est une stratégie intéressante. »**
synergy . . . . synergie

technology . . . . **technologie**
terminology. . . . . terminologie
theology . . . . théologie
toxicology. . . . . toxicologie
trilogy . . . . **trilogie**
typology . . . . typologie

urology . . . . urologie

zoology . . . . zoologie

10A.

Reliez les paires de mots synonymes ou associés.

1. allergie	temps
2. stratégie	pierre
3. psychologie	trois
4. géologie	dynamisme
5. énergie	tactique
6. chronologie	pollen
7. trilogie	mental

10B.

Ecoutez et lisez l'histoire. Répondez aux questions suivantes avec des phrases complètes.

A neuf heures du matin Philippe et Marie vont chez Nicolas. Il vit à Monte-Carlo et c'est un homme très sympathique qui a beaucoup d'énergie. Soudain il dit : « Bonjour les jeunes, est-ce que le café vous donne (gives you) **des allergies ? » Les jeunes disent que non et ils prennent tous un café ensemble. Nicolas commence immédiatement à parler de ses nouvelles technologies médicales et demande à Philippe s'il étudie la radiologie. Philippe dit qu'il n'a jamais étudié** (he never studied) **la radiologie mais qu'il a fait un an** (he did one year) **de biologie. Nicolas demande à Marie si elle étudie la psychologie. Quand elle dit que non, Nicolas dit : « Alors, tu étudies la météorologie ? » Marie regarde Philippe ; il comprend rapidement ce que « différent » veut dire.**

1. Est-ce que Nicolas est paresseux (lazy), ou est-ce qu'il a beaucoup d'énergie ?

2. Est-ce que le café donne des allergies aux jeunes ?

3. De quoi parle Nicolas ?

4. Est-ce que Philippe étudie la radiologie ?

5. Est-ce que Marie étudie la psychologie ?

Chapter 11

English words ending in "–ic" often correspond to "–ique" in French.

French words ending in "–ique" are often adjectives. For example,

an electronic dictionary = *un dictionnaire électronique*

All words and phrases in **bold** *are on* **Track 11** *of the accompanying audio.*

ENGLISH	FRENCH
academic	académique
acoustic	acoustique
acrobatic	acrobatique
acrylic	acrylique
Adriatic	Adriatique
aeronautic	aéronautique
aesthetic	esthétique
agnostic	agnostique
alcoholic	**alcoolique** *(for a cocktail, use "alcoolisé")*
algebraic	algébrique
allergic	**allergique**
alphabetic	alphabétique
anachronistic	anachronique
anemic	anémique
analgesic	analgésique
analytic	analytique
anarchic	anarchique
angelic	angélique
anorexic	anorexique
antarctic	antarctique
antibiotic	antibiotique
antique	antique *(only an adjective)*
antiseptic	antiseptique

apathetic . . . . apathique
apocalyptic. . . . . apocalyptique
aquatic. . . . . aquatique
archaic. . . . . archaïque
arctic . . . . arctique
aristocratic . . . . aristocratique
arithmetic . . . . arithmétique
aromatic. . . . . aromatique
arthritic . . . . arthritique
artistic . . . . **artistique** *(more commonly* "artiste," *for people)*
Asiatic . . . . asiatique
asthmatic . . . . asthmatique
astronomic . . . . astronomique
athletic . . . . **athlétique**
"I'm very athletic." . . . . **« Je suis très athlétique. »**
Atlantic . . . . Atlantique
atmospheric . . . . atmosphérique
atomic . . . . atomique
authentic . . . . **authentique**
autistic . . . . autistique *(more commonly* "autiste," *for people)*
autobiographic . . . . autobiographique
automatic . . . . automatique

ballistic . . . . balistique
balsamic . . . . balsamique
Baltic . . . . Baltique
barometric . . . . barométrique
basic . . . . basique
biographic . . . . biographique
bionic . . . . bionique
botanic. . . . . botanique
bubonic . . . . bubonique
bucolic. . . . . bucolique
bulimic. . . . . boulimique

bureaucratic . . . . bureautique

caloric . . . . calorique
catastrophic . . . . catastrophique
cathartic. . . . . cathartique
Catholic . . . . **Catholique** *(lower case if adjective)*
caustic . . . . caustique
celtic . . . . celtique
ceramic . . . . céramique
characteristic. . . . . caractéristique
charismatic . . . . charismatique
choleric . . . . colérique
chronic. . . . . **chronique**
cinematic . . . . cinématographique
citric . . . . citrique
civic. . . . . civique
classic . . . . **classique**
cleric . . . . ecclésiastique
climatic . . . . climatique
clinic . . . . clinique
comic. . . . . comique
concentric. . . . . concentrique
cosmetic . . . . cosmétique
cosmic . . . . cosmique
critic . . . . critique *(also used for "criticism" and "critical")*
cubic . . . . cubique
cylindric . . . . cylindrique
cynic . . . . cynique
cyrillic . . . . cyrillique

democratic . . . . **démocratique**
demographic . . . . démographique
despotic . . . . despotique
diabetic . . . . diabétique
diabolic . . . . diabolique

diagnostic. . . . . diagnostique
dialectic . . . . dialectique
didactic . . . . didactique
diplomatic . . . . diplomatique
dogmatic . . . . dogmatique
domestic. . . . . **domestique** *(for politics and travel, use "intérieur")*
Doric . . . . dorique
dramatic. . . . . dramatique
drastic . . . . **drastique**
dynamic . . . . dynamique
dyslexic . . . . dyslexique

eccentric. . . . . excentrique
ecclesiastic . . . . ecclésiastique
eclectic. . . . . éclectique
economic . . . . économique
ecstatic. . . . . extatique
egocentric . . . . égocentrique
elastic . . . . élastique
electric . . . . électrique
electromagnetic. . . . . électromagnétique
electronic . . . . **électronique**
"She has an electronic dictionary." . . . **« Elle a un dictionnaire électronique. »**
emblematic . . . . emblématique
emphatic . . . . emphatique
energetic . . . . énergique
enigmatic . . . . énigmatique
epic. . . . . épique
epidemic . . . . épidémique
epileptic . . . . épileptique
erotic . . . . érotique
erratic . . . . erratique *(more commonly "imprévisible")*
esoteric . . . . ésotérique
ethic . . . . éthique

ethnic . . . . ethnique
euphoric . . . . euphorique
evangelic . . . . évangélique
exotic . . . . **exotique**
"I like exotic fruit." . . . . **« J'aime les fruits exotiques. »**

fanatic . . . . fanatique
fantastic . . . . **fantastique**
frenetic . . . . frénétique

gastric . . . . gastrique
geographic . . . . géographique
geologic . . . . géologique
geometric . . . . géométrique
generic . . . . générique
genetic . . . . génétique
geriatric . . . . gériatrique
Germanic . . . . germanique
gothic . . . . gothique

harmonic . . . . harmonique
hedonistic . . . . hédonistique *(more commonly "hedoniste," for people)*
hemispheric . . . . hémisphérique
heretic . . . . hérétique
hermetic . . . . hermétique
heroic . . . . **héroïque**
hierarchic . . . . hiérarchique
hieroglyphic . . . . hiéroglyphique
Hispanic . . . . Hispanique *(only used for Central/South America, lower case if adjective)*
historic . . . . **historique**
"It's a historic date." . . . . **« C'est une date historique. »**
homeopathic . . . . homéopathique
hydraulic . . . . hydraulique

hygienic . . . . hygiénique
hyperbolic . . . . hyperbolique
hypnotic . . . . hypnotique
hypodermic . . . . hypodermique
hysteric . . . . hystérique

idiomatic . . . . idiomatique
idyllic . . . . idyllique
intrinsic . . . . intrinsèque
ionic . . . . ionique
ironic . . . . **ironique**
"It's ironic!" . . . . **« C'est ironique ! »**
Islamic . . . . islamique
isometric . . . . isométrique
italic . . . . italique

Jurassic . . . . jurassique

kinetic . . . . cinétique

laconic . . . . laconique
lactic . . . . lactique
lethargic . . . . léthargique
linguistic . . . . linguistique
lithographic . . . . lithographique
logic . . . . **logique** *(also used for "logical")*
logistic . . . . logistique
lunatic . . . . lunatique *(meaning "moody," or "spaced-out")*
lyric . . . . lyrique

magic . . . . magique *(only an adjective, noun is "magie")*
magnetic . . . . magnétique
mathematic . . . . mathématique(s)
melodramatic . . . . mélodramatique

metalinguistic . . . . métalinguistique
metallic . . . . métallique
metaphoric . . . . métaphorique
metaphysic . . . . métaphysique
methodic . . . . méthodique
metric . . . . **métrique**
"France uses the metric system." . . . . **« La France utilise le système métrique. »**
microscopic . . . . **microscopique**
misanthropic . . . . misanthropique
monarchic . . . . monarchique
mosaic . . . . mosaïque
mnemonic . . . . mnémotechnique
music . . . . musique
mystic . . . . mystique
mythic . . . . mythique

narcissistic . . . . narcissique
narcotic . . . . narcotique
Nordic . . . . nordique
nostalgic . . . . **nostalgique**
"He's very nostalgic." . . . . . . **« Il est très nostalgique. »**
numeric . . . . numérique

oceanic . . . . océanique
olympic . . . . olympique
optic . . . . optique
organic . . . . organique
orgasmic . . . . orgasmique
orthopedic . . . . orthopédique

Pacific . . . . Pacifique
pancreatic . . . . pancréatique
panic . . . . **panique**
panoramic . . . . panoramique
paraplegic . . . . paraplégique

pathetic . . . . **pathétique**
pathologic . . . . pathologique
patriotic . . . . **patriotique**
periodic . . . . périodique
phallic . . . . phallique
philanthropic. . . . . philanthropique
phonetic . . . . phonétique
photogenic . . . . photogénique
photographic . . . . photographique
picnic. . . . . pique-nique
plastic . . . . plastique
platonic . . . . platonique
pneumatic. . . . . pneumatique
poetic. . . . . **poétique**
polemic . . . . polémique
politic. . . . . politique *(only a noun, "policy" or "politics")*
pornographic . . . . pornographique
pragmatic. . . . . pragmatique
prehistoric . . . . préhistorique
problematic . . . . problématique
prolific . . . . prolifique
prophetic . . . . prophétique
prosaic. . . . . prosaïque
prosthetic . . . . prothétique
psychedelic. . . . . psychédélique
psychiatric . . . . psychiatrique
psychic. . . . . psychique
psychotic . . . . psychotique

relic . . . . relique
republic . . . . république
rhetoric . . . . rhétorique
rhythmic . . . . rythmique
romantic. . . . . **romantique**
"It's a romantic story." . . . . . . **« C'est une histoire romantique. »**

rubric . . . . rubrique *(also used for "newspaper column")*
rustic . . . . rustique

sadistic. . . . . sadique
sarcastic . . . . **sarcastique**
sardonic. . . . . sardonique
satanic . . . . satanique
satiric. . . . . satirique
skeptic . . . . sceptique
schematic . . . . schématique
scholastic . . . . scolastique
scientific . . . . **scientifique**
seismic . . . . sismique
semantic. . . . . sémantique
sociolinguistic . . . . sociolinguistique
soporific. . . . . soporifique
spasmodic . . . . spasmodique
specific. . . . . **spécifique**
sporadic. . . . . sporadique
static . . . . statique
statistic. . . . . statistique
stoic. . . . . stoïque
strategic . . . . **stratégique**
stylistic . . . . stylistique
supersonic . . . . supersonique
symbolic. . . . . **symbolique**
symmetric . . . . symétrique
sympathetic. . . . . sympathique
synthetic . . . . synthétique

tactic . . . . tactique
telegenic . . . . télégénique
telegraphic . . . . télégraphique
telepathic . . . . télépathique

telescopic . . . . télescopique
thematic . . . . thématique
theocratic . . . . théocratique
theoretic . . . . théorique
therapeutic . . . . thérapeutique
tonic . . . . tonique
toxic . . . . toxique
tragic . . . . tragique
traumatic . . . . traumatique
tropic . . . . tropique

ultrasonic . . . . ultrasonique

volcanic . . . . volcanique

zoologic . . . . zoologique

Reliez les paires de mots synonymes ou associés.

1. stratégique	sarcastique
2. électronique	date
3. artistique	romain
4. classique	créatif
5. ironique	tactique
6. authentique	radio
7. historique	véritable

11B.

Ecoutez et lisez l'histoire. Répondez aux questions suivantes avec des phrases complètes.

Après deux jours à Monaco, Philippe et Marie vont à Nice. Le centre de Nice est très beau, d'une beauté classique. Pendant la journée ils vont visiter quelques musées artistiques et, le soir, ils voient (they see) **que la ville est magique. Il n'y a pas de raison spécifique, mais Nice est une ville fantastique. Philippe conduit une voiture de location** (a rented car)**, mais il y a beaucoup de circulation. Marie pense que ce n'est pas un plan très stratégique. Elle dit : « Le train est mieux** (is better)**, ce n'est pas très romantique de passer les vacances en voiture. » Philippe répond : « On va voir.... »**

1. Quel type de musées visitent-ils ?

2. Quand est-ce que Nice est magique ?

3. Quel type de ville est Nice ?

4. Quel est le problème quand Philippe conduit ?

5. Selon Marie, qu'est-ce qui n'est pas très romantique ?

Chapter 12

Many English words ending in "–ical" correspond to "–ique" in French.

French words ending in "–ique" are often adjectives. For example,

a <u>botanical</u> garden = *un jardin <u>botanique</u>*

All words and phrases in **bold** *are on* **Track 12** *of the accompanying audio.*

ENGLISH	FRENCH
aeronautical	aéronautique
allegorical	allégorique
alphabetical	**alphabétique**
analytical	analytique
anarchical	anarchique
anatomical	anatomique
angelical	angélique
anthropological	anthropologique
antithetical	antithétique
apolitical	apolitique
archaeological	**archéologique**
astrological	astrologique
astronomical	astronomique
asymmetrical	asymétrique
atypical	atypique
autobiographical	autobiographique
biblical	biblique
bibliographical	bibliographique
biochemical	biochimique
biographical	biographique
biological	**biologique**
botanical	**botanique**

"I visited the botanical gardens." . . . . **« J'ai visité le jardin botanique. »**

categorical . . . . catégorique
chemical. . . . . chimique
chronological . . . . chronologique
classical . . . . classique
clinical . . . . clinique
comical . . . . comique *(also used for "comedian")*
cosmological. . . . . cosmologique
critical . . . . **critique** *(also used for "critic" and "criticism")*
cyclical. . . . . cyclique
cylindrical. . . . . cylindrique
cynical . . . . **cynique**
"Don't be cynical!" . . . . **« Ne sois pas cynique ! »**

diabolical . . . . diabolique
dialectical. . . . . dialectique

ecclesiastical. . . . . ecclésiastique
ecological. . . . . écologique
economical . . . . économique
electrical. . . . . **électrique**
empirical . . . . empirique
ethical . . . . éthique
evangelical . . . . évangélique

fanatical . . . . fanatique

genealogical. . . . . généalogique
geographical . . . . géographique
geological . . . . géologique
geometrical. . . . . géométrique

hierarchical . . . . hiérarchique

historical . . . . historique
hypothetical . . . . hypothétique
hysterical . . . . hystérique

identical . . . . **identique**
"The twins are identical." . . . . **« Les jumeaux sont identiques. »**
ideological . . . . idéologique
illogical . . . . illogique
ironical. . . . . ironique

logical . . . . **logique**
logistical. . . . . logistique
lyrical. . . . . lyrique

magical . . . . **magique**
mathematical . . . . mathématique
mechanical. . . . . mécanique
metaphorical. . . . . métaphorique
metaphysical. . . . . métaphysique
meteorological . . . . météorologique
methodical . . . . méthodique
mystical . . . . mystique
mythical . . . . mythique
mythological. . . . . mythologique

nautical . . . . nautique
neurological . . . . neurologique
numerical . . . . numérique

obstetrical. . . . . obstétrique
optical . . . . optique

pathological . . . . pathologique
pedagogical . . . . pédagogique
periodical. . . . . périodique

pharmaceutical . . . . pharmaceutique
philosophical . . . . philosophique
physical . . . . physique
physiological . . . . physiologique
political . . . . politique
practical . . . . **pratique**
problematical . . . . problématique
psychological . . . . psychologique

rhetorical . . . . rhétorique
rhythmical. . . . . rythmique

sabbatical . . . . sabbatique
satirical . . . . satirique
sociological . . . . sociologique
sociopolitical. . . . . sociopolitique
spherical . . . . sphérique
statistical . . . . statistique
symbolical . . . . symbolique
symmetrical. . . . . symétrique

tactical . . . . tactique
technical. . . . . **technique** *(also used for "technique")*
technological . . . . technologique
theological . . . . théologique
theoretical . . . . théorique
typical . . . . **typique**
"That's typical!" . . . . **« C'est typique ! »**
typographical . . . . typographique
tyrannical . . . . tyrannique

zoological . . . . zoologique

12A.

Reliez les paires de mots synonymes ou associés.

1. typique	humain
2. botanique	moralité
3. pratique	mystique
4. électrique	jardin
5. éthique	lampe
6. biologique	normal
7. magique	rationnel

12B.

Ecoutez et lisez l'histoire. Répondez aux questions suivantes avec des phrases complètes.

Philippe dit : « C'est si beau Nice que nous pouvons passer le mois entier (the whole month) **ici. » Marie comprend mais elle dit : « Non, j'ai l'esprit pratique, nous devons continuer notre voyage de façon logique** (logical manner)**. » Philippe voit qu'elle est très logique maintenant et dit : « Marie, c'est typique, j'admire ton sens pratique ! » Elle répond : « Ne sois pas si critique ! Toi aussi tu veux aller à Marseille, pas vrai ? » Philippe répond : « Tu as raison** (you're right)**, allons à Marseille ! »**

1. Est-ce que Philippe veut rester à Nice ou partir ?

2. De quelle façon Marie veut-elle voyager ?

3. Est-ce que Marie a le sens pratique ?

4. Où est-ce qu'ils vont maintenant ?

5. Que dit Marie de Marseille ?

Chapter 13

Many English words ending in "–id" correspond to "–ide" in French.

French words ending in "–ide" are usually adjectives. For example,

a <u>humid</u> day = *un jour <u>humide</u>*

All words and phrases in **bold** *are on* **Track 13** *of the accompanying audio.*

ENGLISH	FRENCH
acid	acide
antacid	antiacide
arid	aride
avid	avide
candid	candide *(meaning "innocent," "naïve")*
Cupid	cupide
fluid	fluide
frigid	frigide
humid	**humide**
"Today is very humid."	**« Aujourd'hui il fait très humide. »**
hybrid	hybride
insipid	insipide
intrepid	intrépide
invalid	invalide *(meaning "disabled soldier/worker")*
liquid	**liquide**
livid	livide
lucid	lucide

morbid . . . . morbide

placid . . . . placide
putrid . . . . putride

rapid . . . . **rapide**
rigid . . . . **rigide**

solid . . . . solide
sordid . . . . sordide
splendid . . . . **splendide**
stupid . . . . **stupide**

timid . . . . **timide**
"Matthew is very timid." . . . . **« Matthieu est très timide. »**
torrid . . . . torride

valid . . . . **valide**
"Your opinion is valid." . . . . . **« Ton opinion est valide. »**

13A.

Reliez les paires de mots synonymes ou associés.

1. valide	inflexible
2. rigide	réservé
3. acide	idiot
4. liquide	magnifique
5. timide	vrai
6. stupide	citron
7. splendide	fluide

13B.

Ecoutez et lisez l'histoire. Répondez aux questions suivantes avec des phrases complètes.

Pour aller à Marseille, Philippe et Marie décident de louer (rent) **une autre voiture. Marie dit que c'est un plan stupide, mais Philippe pense que c'est un plan splendide. Marie dit : « Mais à Nice, le voyage n'était pas très rapide.... » Philippe dit qu'il préfère conduire quand il fait chaud. Pendant le voyage il fait très humide et, soudain, Philippe devient très pâle et il a mal au ventre** (stomachache)**. Marie ne dit rien et va dans une pharmacie acheter un peu d'antiacide pour Philippe. Le pharmacien dit qu'il doit** (he must) **boire beaucoup de liquide et ne pas manger de nourriture acide.**

1. Que dit Marie du plan d'aller à Marseille en voiture ?

2. Que pense Philippe de son idée ?

3. Quel temps fait-il pendant le voyage ?

4. Le pharmacien dit qu'il doit boire quoi ?

5. Le pharmacien dit qu'il ne doit pas manger quoi ?

Chapter 14

English words ending in "– ism" often correspond to "– isme" in French.

French words ending in "–isme" are usually nouns. For example,

communism = *le communisme*

All words and phrases in **bold** *are on* **Track 14** *of the accompanying audio.*

ENGLISH . . . . FRENCH

activism . . . . activisme
absenteeism . . . . absentéisme
absolutism . . . . absolutisme
alcoholism . . . . **alcoolisme**
"Alcoholism is dangerous." . . **« L'alcoolisme est dangereux. »**
altruism . . . . altruisme
Americanism. . . . . américanisme
anachronism . . . . anachronisme
anarchism. . . . . anarchisme
anglicism . . . . anglicisme
antagonism. . . . . antagonisme
anthropomorphism. . . . . anthropomorphisme
antifascism . . . . **antifascisme**
antiracism. . . . . antiracisme
anti-Semitism. . . . . antisémitisme
aphorism . . . . aphorisme
astigmatism. . . . . astigmatisme
atheism . . . . athéisme
athleticism . . . . **athlétisme**
autism . . . . autisme

behaviorism . . . . behaviorisme
bilingualism . . . . bilinguisme

botulism . . . . botulisme
Buddhism . . . . bouddhisme

cannibalism . . . . cannibalisme
capitalism . . . . **capitalisme**
catechism . . . . catéchisme
Catholicism. . . . . catholicisme
centralism . . . . centralisme
chauvinism . . . . chauvinisme
classicism . . . . classicisme
colonialism . . . . colonialisme
communism . . . . **communisme**
"Communism is a political movement." . . . . **« Le communisme est un mouvement politique. »**
conservatism . . . . conservatisme
cubism . . . . cubisme
cynicism . . . . cynisme

Darwinism . . . . darwinisme
deism. . . . . déisme
despotism . . . . despotisme
determinism . . . . déterminisme
dogmatism . . . . dogmatisme
dualism . . . . dualisme
dynamism. . . . . dynamisme

egoism . . . . égoïsme *(meaning "selfishness")*
elitism . . . . élitisme
eroticism. . . . . érotisme
euphemism . . . . euphémisme
existentialism. . . . . existentialisme
exorcism. . . . . exorcisme
expansionism . . . . expansionnisme
expressionism . . . . expressionnisme
extremism . . . . extrémisme

fanaticism . . . . fanatisme
fascism . . . . **fascisme**
fatalism . . . . fatalisme
favoritism . . . . favoritisme
federalism. . . . . fédéralisme
feminism . . . . **féminisme**
formalism . . . . formalisme
fundamentalism . . . . fondamentalisme
futurism . . . . futurisme

globalism . . . . globalisme

hedonism . . . . hédonisme
heroism . . . . héroïsme
Hinduism . . . . hindouisme
humanism . . . . humanisme
hypnotism . . . . hypnotisme

idealism . . . . idéalisme
imperialism . . . . impérialisme
impressionism . . . . **impressionnisme**
"Impressionism is an artistic movement." . . . . **« L'impressionnisme est un mouvement artistique. »**
individualism. . . . . individualisme
industrialism . . . . industrialisme
internationalism . . . . internationalisme
isolationism. . . . . isolationnisme

journalism. . . . . journalisme
Judaism . . . . judaïsme

legalism . . . . légalisme
Leninism . . . . léninisme
liberalism . . . . libéralisme
lyricism. . . . . lyrisme

magnetism . . . . magnétisme
Marxism. . . . . marxisme
masochism . . . . masochisme
mechanism . . . . **mécanisme**
metabolism . . . . métabolisme
microorganism . . . . microorganisme
minimalism . . . . minimalisme
modernism . . . . modernisme
monotheism . . . . monothéisme
moralism . . . . moralisme

narcissism. . . . . narcissisme
nationalism. . . . . **nationalisme**
naturalism. . . . . naturalisme
Nazism . . . . nazisme
neoclassicism . . . . néoclassicisme
neofascism . . . . néofascisme
neologism. . . . . néologisme
nepotism. . . . . népotisme
nihilism. . . . . nihilisme
nonconformism . . . . non-conformisme
nudism . . . . nudisme

objectivism . . . . objectivisme
opportunism . . . . opportunisme
optimism . . . . **optimisme**
"Optimism is a good thing.". . . **« L'optimisme est une bonne chose. »**
organism . . . . **organisme**

parallelism . . . . parallélisme
patriotism . . . . patriotisme
perfectionism . . . . perfectionnisme
pessimism. . . . . pessimisme
pluralism . . . . pluralisme
polytheism . . . . polythéisme
populism . . . . populisme

positivism	positivisme
postmodernism	postmodernisme
pragmatism	pragmatisme
primitivism	primitivisme
prism	prisme
professionalism	**professionnalisme**
protectionism	protectionnisme
provincialism	provincialisme
purism	purisme
puritanism	puritanisme
racism	**racisme**
"Racism is intolerable."	**« Le racisme est intolérable. »**
radicalism	radicalisme
rationalism	rationalisme
realism	réalisme
regionalism	régionalisme
relativism	relativisme
ritualism	ritualisme
romanticism	romantisme
sadism	sadisme
satanism	satanisme
skepticism	scepticisme
schism	schisme
sensualism	sensualisme
separatism	séparatisme
sexism	sexisme
socialism	**socialisme**
spiritualism	spiritualisme
Stalinism	stalinisme
structuralism	structuralisme
surrealism	surréalisme
syllogism	syllogisme
symbolism	symbolisme

terrorism . . . . **terrorisme**
totalitarianism . . . . totalitarisme
tourism. . . . . **tourisme**
"There's a lot of tourism in France." . . . . **« Il y a beaucoup de tourisme en France. »**
truism. . . . . truisme

vandalism. . . . . vandalisme
verbalism . . . . verbalisme
voyeurism . . . . voyeurisme

Reliez les paires de mots synonymes ou associés.

1. communisme	Karl Marx
2. optimisme	patriotisme
3. impressionisme	bombe
4. féminisme	passeport
5. nationalisme	positif
6. tourisme	femme
7. terrorisme	art

14B.

Ecoutez et lisez l'histoire. Répondez aux questions suivantes avec des phrases complètes.

Après le premier jour à Marseille, Philippe se sent mieux (feels better)**. Il y a beaucoup de tourisme à Marseille et beaucoup d'histoire, mais ils décident de se reposer quelques jours sur la plage. Marie achète un livre sur l'histoire de France qui parle de l'influence du socialisme, du fascisme, et du communisme en France. Le livre décrit le nationalisme français et Marie demande à Philippe ce qu'il pense du** (what he thinks about) **capitalisme. Philippe dit : « Marie, tout ça c'est très intéressant, mais... mangeons une glace** (let's get an ice cream) **! »**

1. Est-ce qu'il y a beaucoup de tourisme à Marseille ?

2. Le livre parle de l'influence de quoi en France ?

3. Que décrit le livre ?

4. Qu'est-ce que Marie demande à Philippe ?

5. Que dit Philippe à la fin ?

Chapter 15

Many English words ending in "–ist" correspond to "–iste" in French.

French words ending in "–iste" are usually nouns. For example,

an artist = *un/une artiste*

All words and phrases in **bold** *are on* **Track 15** *of the accompanying audio.*

ENGLISH . . . . FRENCH

abolitionist . . . . abolitionniste
activist . . . . activiste
alarmist . . . . alarmiste
alchemist . . . . alchimiste
altruist . . . . altruiste
anarchist . . . . anarchiste
anatomist . . . . anatomiste
anesthesiologist . . . . anesthésiste
antagonist . . . . antagoniste
anthropologist . . . . anthropologiste
archivist . . . . archiviste *(also used for "filing clerk")*
artist . . . . **artiste**
"Monet is an incredible artist." . . **« Monet est un artiste incroyable. »**

Baptist . . . . Baptiste
bassist . . . . bassiste
behaviorist . . . . behavioriste
biologist . . . . biologiste
botanist . . . . botaniste
Buddhist . . . . bouddhiste *(uppercase if referring to a person)*

Calvinist . . . . calviniste *(uppercase if referring to a person)*
capitalist. . . . . **capitaliste**
caricaturist . . . . caricaturiste
cellist . . . . violoncelliste
centralist. . . . . centraliste
chemist. . . . . chimiste
colonialist. . . . . colonialiste
communist . . . . **communiste**
conformist. . . . . conformiste
cubist. . . . . cubiste
cyclist. . . . . cycliste

dentist . . . . **dentiste**
"I'm afraid of the dentist." . . . **« J'ai peur du dentiste. »**

ecologist. . . . . écologiste
economist. . . . . économiste
egotist . . . . égoïste
elitist . . . . élitiste
essayist . . . . essayiste
exhibitionist . . . . exhibitionniste
existentialist . . . . existentialiste
exorcist . . . . exorciste
expansionist . . . . expansionniste
extremist. . . . . extrémiste

fascist . . . . fasciste
fatalist . . . . fataliste
federalist . . . . fédéraliste
feminist . . . . féministe
finalist . . . . **finaliste**
florist . . . . **fleuriste**
"I'm going to the florist." . . . . **« Je vais chez le fleuriste. »**
flutist . . . . flûtiste
formalist. . . . . formaliste

fundamentalist. . . . . fondamentaliste
futurist . . . . futuriste

guitarist . . . . **guitariste**

harpist . . . . harpiste
hedonist . . . . hédoniste
humanist. . . . . humaniste

idealist. . . . . **idéaliste**
illusionist . . . . illusionniste
imperialist. . . . . impérialiste
impressionist. . . . . impressionniste
individualist . . . . individualiste
isolationist . . . . isolationniste

journalist . . . . journaliste
jurist. . . . . juriste

Leninist. . . . . léniniste *(uppercase if referring to a person)*
list. **liste**
lobbyist . . . . lobbyiste
loyalist . . . . loyaliste

machinist . . . . machiniste
Marxist . . . . marxiste *(uppercase if referring to a person)*
masochist . . . . masochiste
materialist. . . . . matérialiste
Methodist . . . . méthodiste *(uppercase if referring to a person)*
minimalist. . . . . **minimaliste**
modernist . . . . moderniste
monopolist . . . . monopoliste
moralist . . . . moraliste

nationalist. . . . . nationaliste
naturalist . . . . naturaliste
nihilist . . . . nihiliste
nonconformist . . . . non-conformiste
novelist. . . . . nouvelliste *(meaning "short-story writer")*
nudist. . . . . nudiste
nutritionist . . . . **nutritionniste**

objectivist . . . . objectiviste
optimist . . . . **optimiste**
"She's an optimist." . . . . **« Elle est optimiste. »**
opportunist . . . . opportuniste
organist . . . . organiste

pacifist. . . . . pacifiste
perfectionist . . . . perfectionniste
pessimist . . . . **pessimiste**
pianist . . . . **pianiste**
"My father is a pianist.". . . . . **« Mon père est pianiste. »**
pluralist . . . . pluraliste
populist . . . . populiste
positivist. . . . . positiviste
pragmatist . . . . pragmatiste
prohibitionist. . . . . prohibitionniste
protagonist . . . . protagoniste
purist . . . . puriste

racist . . . . **raciste**
realist. . . . . **réaliste**
"This woman is a realist." . . . **« Cette femme est réaliste. »**
receptionist. . . . . réceptionniste
reformist. . . . . réformiste

sadomasochist . . . . sadomasochiste
secessionist. . . . . sécessionniste
semifinalist . . . . demi-finaliste

separatist . . . . séparatiste
sexist . . . . sexiste
socialist . . . . socialiste
soloist . . . . soliste
specialist . . . . spécialiste
spiritualist . . . . spiritualiste
structuralist . . . . structuraliste
stylist . . . . styliste
surrealist. . . . . surréaliste
symbolist . . . . symboliste

terrorist . . . . **terroriste**
tourist . . . . **touriste**

zoologist . . . . zoologiste

15A.

Reliez les paires de mots synonymes ou associés.

1. artiste	visiteur
2. touriste	peintre
3. pessimiste	compétition
4. optimiste	bouquet
5. dentiste	négatif
6. finaliste	dent
7. fleuriste	positif

15B.

Ecoutez et lisez l'histoire. Répondez aux questions suivantes avec des phrases complètes.

Destination : Montpellier ! Pendant que Philippe et Marie se promènent dans Montpellier ils rencontrent (they meet) **un autre couple de Strasbourg. Le jeune homme est dentiste et la jeune femme est artiste. Les nouveaux amis de Philippe et Marie sont des touristes « professionnels » : ils voyagent beaucoup et ils savent beaucoup de choses** (they know a lot) **sur Montpellier. Marie a une liste de questions et le dentiste peut donner une réponse à chaque question. Ils sont très intelligents mais ils forment un couple étrange** (a strange couple)**. La jeune femme est optimiste alors que son petit ami est pessimiste. Elle est idéaliste et il est réaliste. Le dentiste dit à Philippe et Marie : « Vous voulez aller à Perpignan avec nous ? » Philippe répond : « On va voir.... »**

1. Que fait le jeune homme qu'ils rencontrent ?

2. Est-ce que les nouveaux amis de Philippe et Marie voyagent souvent (often) ?

3. Marie a une liste de quoi ?

4. Comment est le dentiste ?

5. Comment est l'artiste ?

Chapter 16 

English words ending in "–ive" often correspond to "–if " in French.

French words ending in "–if" are usually adjectives. For example,

a <u>creative</u> artist = *un artiste <u>créatif</u>*

If the French adjective is feminine it will end in "–ive," just like the English. For example,

a <u>creative</u> woman = *une femme <u>creative</u>*

All words and phrases in **bold** *are on* **Track 16** *of the accompanying audio.*

ENGLISH . . . . FRENCH

abrasive . . . . abrasif
abusive . . . . abusif
accusative . . . . accusatif
active . . . . **actif**
"My friend is active." . . . . . . **« Mon ami est actif. »**
additive . . . . additif
adhesive. . . . . adhésif
adjective. . . . . **adjectif**
"*Cute* is an adjective.". . . . . . **« *Mignon* est un adjectif. »**
administrative . . . . administratif
adoptive. . . . . adoptif
affective . . . . affectif
affirmative . . . . affirmatif
aggressive . . . . **agressif**
allusive. . . . . allusif
alternative . . . . alternatif
associative . . . . associatif
attentive . . . . attentif

attractive . . . . attractif *(more commonly "*attrayant*" or "*attirant*")*

captive . . . . captif
cognitive . . . . cognitif
cohesive . . . . cohésif
collective . . . . collectif
combative . . . . combatif
commemorative . . . . commémoratif
communicative . . . . communicatif
comparative . . . . comparatif
competitive . . . . **compétitif**
comprehensive . . . . compréhensif *(also used for "understanding")*
compulsive . . . . compulsif
connective . . . . conjonctif
consecutive . . . . **consécutif**
constructive . . . . constructif
contemplative . . . . contemplatif
contraceptive . . . . contraceptif
convulsive . . . . convulsif
cooperative . . . . **coopératif**
corrective . . . . correctif
corrosive . . . . corrosif
creative . . . . **créatif**
"This artist is creative." . . . . . **« Cet artiste est créatif. »**
cumulative . . . . cumulatif
curative . . . . curatif
cursive . . . . cursif *(only used in feminine form, "*cursive*")*

dative . . . . datif
decisive . . . . décisif
declarative . . . . déclaratif
decorative . . . . décoratif
deductive . . . . déductif

defensive . . . . défensif
definitive . . . . **définitif**
degenerative. . . . . dégénératif
demonstrative . . . . démonstratif
depressive . . . . dépressif
descriptive . . . . descriptif
destructive . . . . **destructif**
digestive. . . . . digestif
diminutive. . . . . diminutif
directive . . . . directif *(only used in feminine form, "directive")*
discursive . . . . discursif
distinctive . . . . distinctif

effective . . . . effectif
elective. . . . . électif
evasive. . . . . évasif
excessive . . . . **excessif**
exclusive . . . . exclusif
executive . . . . **exécutif** *(more commonly "cadre")*
exhaustive . . . . exhaustif
expansive. . . . . expansif
expletive. . . . . explétif *(more commonly "juron," for "swear word")*
explosive . . . . explosif
expressive . . . . expressif
extensive . . . . extensif

figurative . . . . figuratif *(more commonly "figuré")*
fugitive. . . . . fugitif
furtive. . . . . furtif

genitive . . . . génitif

hyperactive. . . . . hyperactif

imaginative . . . . **imaginatif**
imitative . . . . imitatif
imperative . . . . impératif
implosive . . . . implosif
impulsive . . . . impulsif
inactive . . . . inactif
incisive. . . . . incisif
indicative . . . . indicatif
infinitive . . . . infinitif
inoffensive . . . . inoffensif
instinctive . . . . instinctif
instructive . . . . instructif
intensive . . . . intensif
interactive . . . . **interactif**
interrogative . . . . interrogatif
intransitive . . . . intransitif
introspective . . . . introspectif
intuitive . . . . intuitif
inventive. . . . . inventif

laxative . . . . laxatif
legislative . . . . législatif
lucrative . . . . lucratif

massive . . . . massif *(also used for "solid")*
meditative. . . . . méditatif
motive . . . . motif
multiplicative. . . . . multiplicatif

narrative. . . . . narratif *(also used for "narration")*
native. . . . . natif
negative . . . . **négatif**
nominative . . . . nominatif

objective. . . . . **objectif**
offensive . . . . **offensif**

oppressive . . . . oppressif

partitive . . . . partitif
passive. . . . . passif
pejorative. . . . . pèjoratif
pensive . . . . pensif
perceptive . . . . perceptif *(more commonly* "perspicace"*)*
permissive . . . . permissif
persuasive . . . . persuasif
plaintive. . . . . plaintif
positive . . . . **positif**
possessive . . . . **possessif**
preparative. . . . . préparatif
preservative . . . . préservatif *(meaning "condom")*
preventive. . . . . préventif
primitive. . . . . **primitif**
productive . . . . **productif**
progressive. . . . . progressif
prohibitive . . . . prohibitif
punitive . . . . punitif

qualitative. . . . . qualitatif
quantitative. . . . . quantitatif

radioactive . . . . radioactif
reactive . . . . réactif
receptive . . . . réceptif
recessive . . . . récessif
regressive. . . . . régressif
relative. . . . . relatif *(only an adjective)*
repetitive . . . . **répétitif**
"This movie is repetitive.". . . . **« Ce film est répétitif. »**
representative . . . . représentatif *(only an adjective)*
repressive. . . . . répressif
respective. . . . . respectif
reproductive . . . . reproductif

repulsive. . . . . répulsif
restrictive . . . . restrictif
retroactive . . . . rétroactif
retrospective . . . . rétrospectif *(only an adjective)*

sedative . . . . sédatif
selective . . . . **sélectif**
speculative . . . . spéculatif
subjective . . . . **subjectif**
subjunctive . . . . subjonctif
substantive . . . . substantif
subversive. . . . . subversif
successive. . . . . successif
suggestive. . . . . suggestif
superlative . . . . superlatif

transitive. . . . . transitif

unproductive. . . . . improductif

vegetative. . . . . végétatif

Reliez les paires de mots synonymes ou associés.

1. consécutif	cause
2. créatif	optimiste
3. positif	artistique
4. exécutif	impartial
5. motif	fataliste
6. négatif	successif
7. objectif	patron

16B.

Ecoutez et lisez l'histoire. Répondez aux questions suivantes avec des phrases complètes.

Philippe trouve la ville de Montpellier absolument fascinante. Il avait entendu (he had heard) **des choses négatives sur Montpellier, mais il voit une région créative et compétitive. Marie a aussi une impression positive de Montpellier. Avant de partir Philippe veut aller voir le village où est né** (was born) **son grand-père. « C'est un bon motif pour y aller » dit Marie. Ils vont à Juvignac, un village pas très actif mais très accueillant** (welcoming)**. Ils passent deux jours consécutifs là-bas.**

1. Qu'est-ce que Philippe avait entendu sur Montpellier ?

2. Que pense Philippe de Montpellier ?

3. Quelle est l'impression de Marie sur Montpellier ?

4. Comment est le village de Juvignac ?

5. Combien de jours est-ce qu'ils passent là-bas ?

Chapter 17

English words ending in "–or" often correspond to "–eur" in French.

French words ending in "–eur" are usually nouns. For example,

an error = *une erreur*

All words and phrases in **bold** *are on* **Track 17** *of the accompanying audio.*

ENGLISH	FRENCH
accelerator	accélérateur
accumulator	accumulateur
actor	**acteur**
adaptor	adaptateur
administrator	administrateur
aggressor	agresseur
agitator	agitateur
alternator	alternateur
ambassador	ambassadeur
anterior	antérieur
applicator	applicateur
ardor	ardeur
auditor	auditeur
author	**auteur**
aviator	aviateur
benefactor	bienfaiteur
calculator	calculateur *(only used for "a calculating person"; for the electronic device, use "calculatrice")*
candor	candeur *(meaning "innocence")*
carburetor	carburateur

censor . . . . censeur
clamor . . . . clameur
collaborator . . . . collaborateur
collector . . . . collectionneur
color . . . . **couleur**
"I like this color." . . . . **« J'aime cette couleur. »**
commentator . . . . commentateur
compressor . . . . compresseur
conductor . . . . conducteur *(for music, use "chef d'orchestre")*
confessor . . . . confesseur
conservator . . . . conservateur
conspirator . . . . conspirateur
coordinator . . . . coordinateur
creator . . . . **créateur**
cultivator . . . . cultivateur
cursor . . . . curseur

debtor . . . . débiteur
decorator . . . . décorateur
demonstrator . . . . démonstrateur *(for political demonstrations, use "manifestant")*
detector . . . . détecteur
detonator . . . . détonateur
detractor . . . . détracteur
dictator . . . . **dictateur**
director . . . . **directeur** *(for movies, use "metteur en scene")*
dishonor . . . . déshonneur
distributor . . . . distributeur
divisor . . . . diviseur
doctor . . . . **docteur**
"I'm going to the doctor." . . . **« Je vais chez le docteur. »**
donor . . . . donateur *(only used in the context of a charity)*

editor . . . . éditeur *(also used for "publisher")*
educator . . . . éducateur
elector . . . . électeur
emperor . . . . empereur
equator . . . . équateur
error . . . . **erreur**
"There is an error." . . . . **« Il y a une erreur. »**
excavator . . . . excavateur
executor . . . . exécuteur
exterior . . . . **extérieur**

factor . . . . facteur *(also used for "postman")*
favor . . . . **faveur**
fervor . . . . ferveur

generator . . . . générateur
gladiator . . . . gladiateur
governor . . . . gouverneur

honor . . . . honneur
horror . . . . **horreur**
"It's a horror movie." . . . . **« C'est un film d'horreur. »**
humor . . . . humeur *(meaning "mood")*

illustrator . . . . illustrateur
imitator . . . . imitateur
impersonator . . . . imitateur
impostor . . . . imposteur
incinerator . . . . incinérateur
incubator . . . . incubateur
indicator . . . . indicateur
inferior . . . . **inférieur** *(also used for "lower")*
innovator . . . . **innovateur**
inspector . . . . inspecteur
instigator . . . . instigateur

instructor . . . . instructeur
interior . . . . **intérieur**
interlocutor . . . . interlocuteur
interrogator. . . . . interrogateur
interruptor. . . . . interrupteur *(also used for "electrical switch")*
inventor . . . . **inventeur**
investor . . . . investisseur

labor . . . . labeur
languor . . . . langueur
legislator . . . . législateur
liberator . . . . libérateur
liquidator . . . . liquidateur
liquor. . . . . liqueur *(meaning "liqueur")*

major. . . . . majeur *(also used for "over 18 years old")*
manipulator . . . . manipulateur
mediator. . . . . médiateur
minor . . . . mineur
moderator . . . . modérateur *(more commonly "animateur")*
monitor . . . . moniteur *(also used for "coach")*
monsignor . . . . monseigneur
motor . . . . **moteur**

narrator . . . . narrateur
navigator . . . . navigateur
negotiator. . . . . négociateur

odor . . . . **odeur** *(also used for "scent")*
operator . . . . opérateur
oppressor . . . . oppresseur
orator. . . . . orateur

pallor . . . . pâleur
pastor . . . . pasteur
persecutor. . . . . persécuteur
possessor . . . . possesseur
posterior. . . . . postérieur
precursor . . . . précurseur
predator. . . . . prédateur
predecessor . . . . prédécesseur
professor . . . . **professeur** *(also used for "teacher")*
"My aunt is a professor." . . . . **« Ma tante est professeur. »**
projector . . . . projecteur
prosecutor . . . . procureur
prospector . . . . prospecteur
protector . . . . **protecteur**

radiator . . . . radiateur
rancor . . . . rancœur
reactor . . . . réacteur
receptor . . . . récepteur
reflector . . . . réflecteur
refrigerator . . . . réfrigérateur
regulator . . . . régulateur
respirator . . . . respirateur
rigor . . . . rigueur
rumor. . . . . rumeur *(also used for "low noise," "murmur")*

savior. . . . . sauveur
savor . . . . saveur
sculptor . . . . sculpteur
sector. . . . . secteur
selector . . . . sélecteur
semiconductor. . . . . semi-conducteur
senator. . . . . **sénateur**
"My uncle is a senator." . . . . **« Mon oncle est sénateur. »**
separator . . . . séparateur

simulator . . . . simulateur
solicitor . . . . solliciteur
spectator . . . . spectateur
speculator. . . . . spéculateur
splendor. . . . . splendeur
stupor. . . . . stupeur *(also used for "amazement")*
successor . . . . successeur
superior . . . . supérieur *(also used for "upper")*

tailor . . . . tailleur
terror . . . . **terreur**
torpor. . . . . torpeur
tractor . . . . tracteur
transgressor . . . . transgresseur
translator . . . . traducteur
tumor. . . . . **tumeur**
tutor. . . . . tuteur *(meaning "guardian")*

ulterior . . . . ultérieur *(meaning "subsequent")*

valor . . . . valeur
vendor . . . . vendeur
ventilator . . . . ventilateur *(meaning "electrical fan")*
violator. . . . . violateur
visitor. . . . . visiteur
vapor. . . . . **vapeur** *(also used for "steam")*

17A.

Reliez les paires de mots synonymes ou associés

1. docteur	université
2. acteur	innovateur
3. sénateur	peur
4. professeur	médecin
5. inventeur	voiture
6 moteur	théâtre
7. terreur	congrès

17B.

Ecoutez et lisez l'histoire. Répondez aux questions suivantes avec des phrases complètes.

Dès qu'ils (as soon as) **arrivent à Toulouse, l'oncle leur dit qu'il y aura une fête** (a party) **chez lui ce soir. Marie remarque immédiatement la terreur sur le visage de Philippe. Quand ils sont seuls, Philippe dit : « Quelle erreur de venir ici ! Fais-moi une faveur : dis-moi que je n'ai pas besoin d'aller à cette fête. » Marie ne répond même pas** (doesn't even respond) **et Philippe comprend qu'il doit y aller. La « fête » est très difficile pour Philippe. Toutes les deux minutes, l'oncle dit : « Cet homme est docteur, celui-là** (that one) **est professeur, l'autre est inventeur. » Pendant un moment, Philippe est intéressé quand l'oncle lui dit : « Le sénateur va venir avec un acteur très célèbre. » Mais l'acteur n'est pas célèbre et le sénateur est très, très vieux.**

1. Que remarque Marie sur le visage de Philippe ?

2. Que dit Philippe sur la décision d'aller à Toulouse ?

3. Que dit Philippe sur la fête ?

4. Est-ce que l'acteur est célèbre ?

5. Est-ce que le sénateur est jeune ?

Chapter 18

English words ending in "–ory" generally correspond to "–oire" in French.

French words ending in "–oire" can be nouns or adjectives. For example,

an accessory (n.) = *un accessoire*
contradictory (adj.) = *contradictoire*

All words and phrases in **bold** *are on* **Track 18** *of the accompanying audio.*

ENGLISH . . . . FRENCH

accessory . . . . **accessoire**
ambulatory . . . . ambulatoire

circulatory . . . . circulatoire
compensatory . . . . compensatoire
conservatory . . . . conservatoire
contradictory . . . . **contradictoire**
"That's contradictory!" . . . . . . **« C'est contradictoire ! »**
crematory . . . . crématoire

declaratory . . . . déclaratoire
derisory . . . . dérisoire
derogatory . . . . dérogatoire
discriminatory . . . . discriminatoire

exploratory . . . . exploratoire

glory . . . . gloire

hallucinatory . . . . hallucinatoire
history . . . . histoire

illusory . . . . illusoire
inflammatory. . . . . inflammatoire
interrogatory. . . . . interrogatoire
ivory . . . . ivoire

laboratory . . . . **laboratoire**
"She works in a laboratory." . . . **« Elle travaille dans un laboratoire. »**

memory . . . . mémoire
migratory . . . . migratoire

obligatory . . . . **obligatoire**
observatory . . . . observatoire
oratory. . . . . oratoire

peremptory. . . . . péremptoire
preparatory . . . . préparatoire
promontory. . . . . promontoire
purgatory. . . . . **purgatoire**

refectory. . . . . réfectoire
repertory . . . . répertoire
respiratory . . . . respiratoire

suppository. . . . . suppositoire

territory . . . . **territoire**
"That's his territory." . . . . **« C'est son territoire. »**
trajectory . . . . trajectoire
transitory . . . . transitoire

victory . . . . victoire

Reliez les paires de mots synonymes ou associés.

1. territoire	nécessaire
2. accessoire	zone
3. contradictoire	gagner
4. laboratoire	éléphant
5. obligatoire	ceinture
6. ivoire	recherche
7. victoire	paradoxal

18B.

Ecoutez et lisez l'histoire. Répondez aux questions suivantes avec des phrases complètes.

Philippe est très content quand ils partent finalement de Toulouse pour Bordeaux. Il dit : « J'aurais préféré (I'd have preferred) **une auberge** (a hostel)**. » Marie admet que c'était une <u>histoire</u> étrange. Philippe dit : « Mais, qu'est-ce que tu dis ? C'était pire que le <u>purgatoire</u> ! » Marie répond : « Tu n'avais pas besoin de** (you didn't have to) **venir, ce n'était pas <u>obligatoire</u>. » Philippe rit de ce commentaire <u>contradictoire</u> mais ne répond pas. Philippe dit : « Alors tu me dois une faveur, pas vrai ? » Marie dit : « On va voir.... »**

1. Où vont-ils après Toulouse ?

2. Qu'est-ce que Philippe aurait préféré ?

3. Philippe dit que la fête était pire que quoi ?

4. Est-il vrai que sa présence n'était pas obligatoire ?

5. Est-ce que Philippe répond au dernier commentaire contradictoire de Marie ?

Chapter 19

English words ending in "–ous" generally correspond to "–eux" in French.

French words ending in "–eux" are usually adjectives. For example,

a <u>delicious</u> dinner = *un dîner <u>délicieux</u>*

If the French adjective is feminine, it will end in "–euse." For example,

a <u>delicious</u> pie = une tarte <u>délicieuse</u>

All words and phrases in **bold** *are on* **Track 19** *of the accompanying audio.*

ENGLISH . . . . FRENCH

advantageous . . . . avantageux
adventurous . . . . aventureux
ambitious . . . . **ambitieux**
"My brother is ambitious." . . . **« Mon frère est ambitieux. »**
amorous . . . . amoureux
aqueous . . . . aqueux
audacious. . . . . audacieux

cancerous. . . . . cancéreux
capricious. . . . . capricieux
cavernous. . . . . caverneux
ceremonious . . . . cérémonieux
conscientious . . . . consciencieux
contagious . . . . contagieux
copious . . . . copieux
courageous. . . . . courageux
curious . . . . **curieux**

dangerous . . . . dangereux

delicious . . . . **délicieux**
"This dinner is delicious." . . . . **« Ce dîner est délicieux. »**
desirous . . . . désireux
disastrous . . . . **désastreux**
dubious . . . . douteux

envious . . . . envieux

fabulous . . . . fabuleux
facetious. . . . . facétieux
famous . . . . fameux *(more commonly "célèbre," for people)*
fastidious . . . . fastidieux *(meaning "boring," "tiresome")*
ferrous . . . . ferreux
fibrous . . . . fibreux
furious . . . . **furieux**

gaseous . . . . gazeux
gelatinous. . . . . gélatineux
generous . . . . **généreux**
"My friend is generous." . . . . **« Mon ami est généreux. »**
glorious . . . . glorieux
gracious . . . . gracieux *(meaning "graceful")*

harmonious. . . . . harmonieux
hideous . . . . hideux

ignominious . . . . ignominieux
imperious . . . . impérieux *(also used for "urgent")*
impetuous. . . . . impétueux
incestuous. . . . . incestueux
industrious . . . . industrieux *(more commonly "diligent")*
infectious . . . . infectieux
ingenious . . . . ingénieux
injurious . . . . injurieux

insidious . . . . insidieux
intravenous . . . . intraveineux

joyous . . . . joyeux
judicious . . . . judicieux

laborious . . . . laborieux
licentious . . . . licencieux
litigious . . . . litigieux
luminous . . . . lumineux
luxurious . . . . luxueux

marvelous . . . . merveilleux
melodious . . . . mélodieux
meticulous . . . . méticuleux
miraculous . . . . miraculeux
monstrous . . . . monstrueux
mountainous . . . . montagneux
mysterious . . . . mystérieux

nebulous . . . . nébuleux
nervous . . . . nerveux
numerous . . . . nombreux

oblivious . . . . oublieux
obsequious . . . . obséquieux
odious . . . . odieux
onerous . . . . onéreux *(meaning "costly," "expensive")*
outrageous . . . . outrageux *(more commonly "scandaleux")*

perilous . . . . périlleux
pernicious . . . . pernicieux
pious . . . . pieux
piteous . . . . piteux

pompous . . . . pompeux
populous . . . . populeux
porous . . . . poreux
precious . . . . **précieux**
"This jewelry is precious." . . . **« Ce bijou est précieux. »**
prestigious . . . . **prestigieux**
pretentious . . . . prétentieux
prodigious . . . . prodigieux

religious . . . . **religieux**
"That man is religious." . . . . . **« Cet homme est religieux. »**
rigorous . . . . rigoureux
ruinous . . . . ruineux

scandalous . . . . **scandaleux**
scrupulous . . . . scrupuleux
seditious . . . . séditieux
sentencious . . . . sentencieux
serious . . . . sérieux
sinuous . . . . sinueux
spacious . . . . **spacieux**
"My apartment is spacious." . . . **« Mon appartement est spacieux. »**
specious . . . . spécieux
studious . . . . studieux
sumptuous . . . . somptueux
superstitious . . . . superstitieux

tortuous . . . . **tortueux**
tumultuous . . . . tumultueux

unctuous . . . . onctueux
ungracious . . . . disgracieux

vaporous . . . . vaporeux
venomous . . . . venimeux
vicious . . . . vicieux *(more commonly* "méchant"*)*

victorious . . . . victorieux
vigorous . . . . vigoureux
virtuous . . . . **vertueux**
viscous . . . . visqueux
voluptuous . . . . voluptueux

19A.

Reliez les paires de mots synonymes ou associés.

1. spacieux	fameux
2. ambitieux	appétissant
3. curieux	charitable
4. délicieux	déterminé
5. prestigieux	vaste
6. nerveux	émotionnel
7. généreux	inquisiteur

19B.

Ecoutez et lisez l'histoire. Répondez aux questions suivantes avec des phrases complètes.

Après la visite désastreuse à Toulouse, les deux voyageurs sont prêts pour une fin de semaine ambitieuse à Bordeaux. Marie sait que cet endroit est célèbre pour ses cannelés[1] **délicieux, mais elle n'en sait pas beaucoup plus sur la ville. Philippe est aussi très curieux de connaître Bordeaux. Son ami lui a dit** (told him) **qu'il y a un air mystérieux là-bas. A l'université de Bordeaux il y a un programme prestigieux de langues étrangères. Marie dit : « Quiconque étudie** (whoever studies) **à l'étranger doit être ambitieux. » Ils logent dans un hôtel très spacieux et ils y sont** (they find it) **très bien. Avant de partir pour Limoges, Marie dit : « J'aime beaucoup Bordeaux, mais ce n'est pas un endroit mystérieux, peut-être que ton ami est un type nerveux ! »**

[1] Individual bell-shaped cake/flan, specialty of Bordeaux

1. Comment a été la visite de Toulouse ?

2. Comment sont les cannelés de Bordeaux ?

3. Qu'est-ce que l'ami de Philippe a dit sur cette ville ?

4. Quel est le programme prestigieux à l'université de Bordeaux ?

5. Comment est leur hôtel ?

Chapter 20

Many English words ending in "–sion" have the same ending in French.

French words ending in "–sion" are usually feminine nouns. For example,

a session = *une session*

All words and phrases in **bold** *are on* **Track 20** *of the accompanying audio.*

ENGLISH . . . . FRENCH

adhesion . . . . adhésion *(also used for "membership")*
admission. . . . . admission *(more commonly "*entrée*")*
aggression . . . . agression
allusion . . . . allusion
apprehension . . . . appréhension
ascension . . . . ascension
aversion . . . . aversion

circumcision . . . . circoncision
cohesion. . . . . cohésion
collision . . . . **collision**
collusion. . . . . collusion
commission. . . . . commission
compassion . . . . compassion
comprehension . . . . **compréhension**
compression . . . . compression
compulsion . . . . compulsion
concession . . . . concession
conclusion. . . . . **conclusion**
confession . . . . confession
confusion . . . . **confusion**
"There's a lot of confusion." . . **« Il y a beaucoup de confusion. »**
contusion . . . . contusion

conversion . . . . conversion
convulsion . . . . convulsion
corrosion . . . . corrosion

decision . . . . **décision**
"It's an important decision." . . . **« C'est une décision importante. »**
decompression . . . . décompression
depression . . . . dépression *(also used for "nervous breakdown")*
derision . . . . dérision
diffusion . . . . diffusion
digression. . . . . digression
dimension. . . . . **dimension**
discussion. . . . . discussion *(also used for "argument")*
disillusion . . . . désillusion
dispersion. . . . . dispersion
dissension. . . . . dissension
dissuasion . . . . dissuasion
diversion . . . . diversion
division . . . . **division**

effusion . . . . effusion
elision . . . . élision
emission . . . . émission *(also used for "TV/radio show")*
erosion. . . . . érosion
evasion . . . . évasion *(meaning "escape")*
exclusion . . . . exclusion
excursion . . . . excursion
expansion. . . . . expansion
explosion . . . . **explosion**
expression . . . . **expression**
expulsion . . . . expulsion
extension . . . . extension
extroversion . . . . extraversion

fission . . . . fission

fusion . . . . fusion *(meaning "merger")*

hypertension . . . . hypertension

illusion . . . . illusion
immersion. . . . . immersion
implosion . . . . implosion
imprecision. . . . . imprécision
impression . . . . **impression**
"He made a good impression." . . . **« Il a fait bonne impression. »**
impulsion . . . . impulsion
incision . . . . incision
inclusion. . . . . inclusion
incomprehension . . . . incompréhension
incursion . . . . incursion
indecision. . . . . indécision
infusion . . . . infusion *(also used for "herbal tea")*
intercession. . . . . intercession
intermission. . . . . intermission *(for shows/theater, use "entracte")*
introversion. . . . . introversion
intrusion . . . . intrusion
invasion . . . . invasion
inversion. . . . . inversion

lesion . . . . lésion

mission. . . . . **mission**

obsession . . . . obsession
occasion. . . . . occasion *(also used for "opportunity," and as an adjective, "secondhand")*
omission. . . . . omission
oppression . . . . oppression

passion . . . . **passion**

"It's my passion." . . . . **« C'est ma passion. »**

pension . . . . pension *(also used for "small hotel")*

percussion . . . . percussion

permission . . . . permission

persuasion . . . . persuasion

perversion . . . . perversion

possession . . . . possession

precision. . . . . **précision**

pretension. . . . . prétention

prevision . . . . prévision *(meaning "forecast")*

procession . . . . procession

profession. . . . . **profession**

profusion . . . . profusion

progression. . . . . progression

propulsion . . . . propulsion

provision . . . . provision

recession . . . . récession

regression. . . . . régression

remission . . . . rémission

repercussion . . . . répercussion

repression. . . . . répression

repulsion . . . . répulsion

revision . . . . révision

secession . . . . sécession

session . . . . **session**

subdivision . . . . subdivision

submersion . . . . submersion

submission . . . . soumission

subversion . . . . subversion

succession . . . . succession *(also used for "inheritance")*

supervision . . . . supervision

suppression. . . . . suppression

suspension . . . . suspension

television . . . . **télévision**
tension . . . . **tension**
transfusion . . . . transfusion
transgression. . . . . transgression
transmission . . . . transmission

version . . . . version
vision . . . . **vision**

20A.

Reliez les paires de mots synonymes ou associés.

1. mission	impact
2. confusion	objectif
3. collision	chaos
4. tension	bombe
5. télévision	exactitude
6. précision	film
7. explosion	anxiété

20B.

Ecoutez et lisez l'histoire. Répondez aux questions suivantes avec des phrases complètes.

Dès qu'ils arrivent à Limoges, Marie déclare : « Nous avons une mission claire ici à Limoges. Tu sais que la porcelaine est une de mes passions, pas vrai ? Je dois trouver une nouvelle assiette (plate) **en porcelaine pour ma collection. » Philippe dit : « Très bien, mais peut-être que nous pouvons la trouver à Versailles ? » Marie insiste : « Non ! Ma décision finale est prise ! Je veux une assiette de Limoges. » Philippe a l'impression que Marie ne plaisante pas** (isn't kidding around) **et il s'applique à la « mission de l'assiette. » Après un déjeuner fabuleux sur la place ils partent en chasse** (the hunt)**. Il y avait un peu de confusion avec toutes les rues et les impasses, mais finalement il y a une conclusion heureuse : Marie trouve son assiette.**

1. Quelle est la mission de Marie ?

2. Pourquoi est-ce qu'elle veut cette chose ?

3. Que dit Marie de sa décision ?

4. Quelle impression Philippe a-t-il de Marie ?

5. Pourquoi est-ce qu'il y avait un peu de confusion ?

Chapter 21

English words ending in "–sis" generally correspond to "–se" in French.

French words ending in "–se" are usually feminine nouns. For example,

a crisis = *une crise*

All words and phrases in **bold** *are on* **Track 21** *of the accompanying audio.*

ENGLISH . . . . FRENCH

analysis . . . . **analyse**
antithesis . . . . antithèse

basis . . . . base
biogenesis . . . . biogenèse

catalysis . . . . catalyse
cirrhosis . . . . cirrhose
crisis . . . . **crise**
"The economy is in a crisis." . . . **« L'économie est en crise. »**

dialysis . . . . **dialyse**

electrolysis . . . . électrolyse
emphasis . . . . **emphase** *(only used for speech)*

genesis . . . . **genèse**

hydrolysis . . . . hydrolyse
hypnosis . . . . **hypnose**
hypothesis . . . . **hypothèse**
"The hypothesis is interesting." . . **« L'hypothèse est intéressante. »**

metamorphosis . . . . **métamorphose**
metastasis. . . . . métastase
microanalysis . . . . microanalyse
mitosis . . . . mitose
mononucleosis. . . . . mononucléose
mycosis . . . . mycose

narcosis . . . . narcose
neurosis . . . . névrose

osmosis . . . . osmose
osteoporosis . . . . ostéoporose

parenthesis . . . . parenthèse
photogenesis. . . . . photogenése
photosynthesis. . . . . photosynthèse
psychoanalysis . . . . psychanalyse
psychosis . . . . psychose

sclerosis . . . . sclérose
scoliosis . . . . scoliose
self-analysis . . . . auto-analyse
self-hypnosis . . . . auto-hypnose
synthesis. . . . . synthèse

thesis . . . . **thèse**
"I'm writing my thesis." . . . . . **« J'écris ma thèse. »**
tuberculosis. . . . . tuberculose

21A.

Reliez les paires de mots synonymes ou associés.

1. métamorphose	pendule
2. analyse	changement
3. crise	sang
4. emphase	étude
5. hypothèse	présomption
6. dialyse	problème
7. hypnose	accentuation

21B.

Ecoutez et lisez l'histoire. Répondez aux questions suivantes avec des phrases complètes.

Destination : Tours ! Philippe et Marie connaissent déjà (already know) **Tours assez bien. Alors ils ne mettent pas vraiment l'accent sur la ballade touristique. Au lieu de ça** (instead)**, ils vont chercher un cousin de Philippe qui étudie à Tours. Il s'appelle Charles et étudie l'économie. Il écrit sa <u>thèse</u> sur la <u>crise</u> financière du tiers-monde** (of the Third World)**. Charles dit : « Malheureusement, je n'ai pas ma propre <u>hypothèse</u> sur la façon d'arrêter la <u>crise</u> et... sans cette <u>hypothèse</u>, je ne peux pas faire ma <u>thèse</u> ! » Charles demande à Philippe : « Est-ce que tu peux m'aider ? » Philippe répond : « On va voir.... »**

1. Pourquoi est-ce qu'ils ne mettent pas vraiment l'accent sur la ballade touristique à Tours ?

2. Qu'est-qu'ils font alors à Tours?

3. Sur quoi Charles écrit-il sa thèse ?

4. Charles a-t-il une bonne hypothèse pour sa thèse ?

5. Qu'est-ce que Charles demande à Philippe ?

Chapter 22

Many English words ending in "–tion" have the same ending in French.

French words ending in "–tion" are usually feminine nouns. For example,

a celebration = *une célébration*

All words and phrases in **bold** *are on* **Track 22** *of the accompanying audio.*

ENGLISH . . . . FRENCH

abbreviation . . . . abréviation
abdication . . . . abdication
aberration . . . . aberration
abjection . . . . abjection
abnegation . . . . abnégation
abolition. . . . . abolition
abomination . . . . abomination
absolution. . . . . absolution
absorption . . . . absorption
abstention. . . . . abstention
abstraction . . . . abstraction
acceleration . . . . accélération
acclamation . . . . acclamation
accreditation. . . . . accréditation
accommodation. . . . . accommodation *(meaning "adjustment," or "arrangement," not "hotel accommodation")*
accumulation . . . . accumulation
accusation . . . . accusation
acquisition . . . . acquisition
action. . . . . **action** *(also used for "stock share")*
activation . . . . activation
adaptation . . . . adaptation

addition . . . . addition *(also used for "bill," "check")*
administration . . . . administration
admiration . . . . admiration
adoption . . . . adoption
adoration . . . . adoration
adulation . . . . adulation
affection . . . . affection
affiliation . . . . affiliation
affirmation . . . . affirmation
affliction . . . . affliction
agglomeration. . . . . agglomération
aggravation . . . . aggravation *(meaning "worsening")*
agitation. . . . . agitation
alienation . . . . aliénation
alimentation . . . . alimentation
allegation . . . . allégation
alliteration . . . . allitération
allocation . . . . allocation
alteration . . . . altération
altercation . . . . altercation
ambition. . . . . **ambition**
"She has ambition." . . . . **« Elle a de l'ambition. »**
amelioration . . . . amélioration
amputation . . . . amputation
animation . . . . animation
annihilation. . . . . annihilation
annotation . . . . annotation
anticipation . . . . anticipation
apparition . . . . apparition
application . . . . application *(for "application form," use* "formulaire"*)*
appreciation . . . . appréciation *(also used for "evaluation," "judgment")*
approximation . . . . approximation
articulation . . . . articulation
aspiration . . . . aspiration

assertion . . . . assertion
assimilation. . . . . assimilation
association . . . . association
attention. . . . . **attention** *(also used for "look out!")*
attenuation . . . . atténuation
attraction . . . . attraction
attribution. . . . . attribution
audition . . . . audition
augmentation . . . . augmentation
authorization. . . . . autorisation
automation . . . . automatisation
aviation . . . . aviation *(also used for "air force")*

bastion. . . . . bastion
benediction. . . . . bénédiction

capitalization . . . . capitalisation
capitulation. . . . . capitulation
castration . . . . castration
celebration . . . . **célébration** *(for "party," use "fête")*
"The (religious) celebration is tomorrow." . . . . **« La célébration a lieu demain. »**
centralization . . . . centralisation
certification. . . . . certification
cessation . . . . cessation
circulation. . . . . circulation *(also used for "traffic")*
circumspection . . . . circonspection
citation. . . . . citation *(also used for "quotation")*
civilization . . . . civilisation
classification . . . . classification
coagulation . . . . coagulation
coalition . . . . coalition
cohabitation . . . . cohabitation
collaboration . . . . collaboration
collection . . . . **collection**
colonization . . . . colonisation

coloration . . . . coloration
combination . . . . combinaison
combustion . . . . combustion
commemoration. . . . . commémoration
commercialization . . . . commercialisation
commiseration. . . . . commisération
commotion . . . . commotion *(meaning "concussion")*
communication . . . . communication *(also used for "phone call")*
compensation . . . . compensation
competition. . . . . compétition
compilation. . . . . compilation
complication . . . . complication
composition . . . . composition
concentration . . . . concentration
conception . . . . conception
conciliation. . . . . conciliation
condemnation . . . . condamnation
condensation . . . . condensation
condition . . . . **condition**
confection. . . . . confection
confederation . . . . confédération
configuration. . . . . configuration
confirmation . . . . confirmation
confiscation . . . . confiscation
confrontation. . . . . confrontation
congestion . . . . congestion
congregation . . . . congrégation
conjugation. . . . . conjugaison
conjunction . . . . conjonction
connotation. . . . . connotation
conscription . . . . conscription
consecration . . . . consécration
conservation . . . . conservation
consideration . . . . considération
consolation . . . . consolation

consolidation . . . . consolidation
constellation . . . . constellation
consternation . . . . consternation
constipation . . . . constipation
constitution . . . . constitution
construction . . . . construction
consultation . . . . consultation
consumption . . . . consommation
contamination . . . . contamination
contemplation . . . . contemplation
continuation . . . . continuation
contraception . . . . contraception
contraction . . . . contraction
contradiction. . . . . contradiction
contribution. . . . . contribution
contrition . . . . contrition
convection . . . . convection
convention . . . . convention
conversation . . . . **conversation**
"His conversation is fascinating." . . . . **« Sa conversation est fascinante. »**
conviction. . . . . conviction
convocation . . . . convocation
cooperation . . . . coopération
coordination . . . . **coordination**
copulation . . . . copulation
corporation. . . . . corporation
correction . . . . correction
correlation . . . . corrélation
corruption. . . . . corruption
creation . . . . création
cremation . . . . crémation

damnation . . . . damnation
decapitation . . . . décapitation
deceleration . . . . décélération

deception . . . . déception *(meaning "disappointment")*
declaration . . . . déclaration
decomposition. . . . . décomposition
decoration . . . . décoration
deduction . . . . déduction
defection . . . . défection *(also used for "cancellation")*
definition . . . . **définition**
deflation. . . . . déflation *(only used in an economic context)*
deformation . . . . déformation
degradation . . . . dégradation
dehydration . . . . déshydratation
delegation . . . . délégation
deliberation . . . . délibération
demarcation . . . . démarcation
demolition . . . . démolition
demonstration . . . . démonstration
denomination . . . . dénomination
denunciation. . . . . dénonciation
deportation. . . . . déportation
deposition . . . . déposition
depreciation . . . . dépréciation
deprivation . . . . privation
derivation . . . . dérivation
description . . . . description
designation. . . . . désignation
desolation. . . . . désolation
destabilization . . . . déstabilisation
destination . . . . destination
destitution. . . . . destitution *(meaning "dismissal")*
destruction . . . . **destruction**
detection . . . . détection
detention . . . . détention
deterioration . . . . détérioration
determination . . . . détermination
detonation . . . . détonation

devaluation	dévaluation
devastation	dévastation
deviation	déviation
devotion	dévotion *(only used in a religious context)*
diction	diction
differentiation	différentiation
digestion	digestion
dilution	dilution
direction	**direction**
discoloration	décoloration
discretion	discrétion
discrimination	discrimination
disinfection	désinfection
disintegration	désintégration
disposition	disposition
disqualification	disqualification
dissection	dissection
dissertation	dissertation
dissimulation	dissimulation
dissipation	dissipation
dissociation	dissociation
dissolution	dissolution
distillation	distillation
distinction	distinction
distraction	distraction
distribution	distribution
diversification	diversification
documentation	documentation
domination	domination
dramatization	dramatisation *(also used for "exaggeration")*
edification	édification
edition	**édition**
education	éducation

ejaculation . . . . éjaculation
ejection . . . . éjection
elaboration . . . . élaboration
election . . . . élection
electrocution . . . . électrocution
elevation . . . . élévation
elimination . . . . élimination
elocution . . . . élocution
elongation . . . . élongation
elucidation . . . . élucidation
emanation . . . . émanation
emancipation . . . . émancipation
emigration . . . . émigration
emotion . . . . **émotion**
emulation . . . . émulation
enumeration . . . . énumération
enunciation . . . . énonciation
equation . . . . équation
eradication . . . . éradication
erection . . . . érection
erudition . . . . érudition
eruption . . . . éruption
estimation . . . . estimation
evacuation . . . . évacuation
evaluation . . . . évaluation
evaporation . . . . évaporation
eviction . . . . éviction
evocation . . . . évocation
evolution . . . . évolution
exaggeration . . . . **exagération**
"That's an exaggeration." . . . **« C'est une exagération. »**
exasperation . . . . exaspération
excavation . . . . excavation
exception . . . . exception
exclamation . . . . exclamation
excretion . . . . excrétion

execution . . . . exécution
exemption. . . . . exemption
exhibition . . . . exposition
exhortation . . . . exhortation
exoneration . . . . exonération
expedition . . . . expédition *(also used for "sending," "shipping")*
experimentation. . . . . expérimentation
expiration. . . . . expiration
explanation . . . . explication
exploitation. . . . . exploitation
exploration . . . . exploration
exportation . . . . exportation
exposition. . . . . exposition
extermination . . . . extermination
extinction . . . . extinction
extraction . . . . extraction
extradition . . . . extradition
exultation . . . . exultation

fabrication . . . . fabrication *(meaning "manufacturing")*
faction . . . . faction
falsification . . . . falsification
fascination . . . . fascination
federation. . . . . fédération *(meaning "league")*
fermentation . . . . fermentation
fertilization . . . . fertilisation
fiction. . . . . fiction
filtration . . . . filtration
fixation. . . . . fixation
flagellation . . . . flagellation
fluctuation. . . . . fluctuation
formation . . . . formation *(also used for "training")*
formulation . . . . formulation
fornication . . . . fornication
fortification . . . . fortification

foundation . . . . **fondation**
fraction . . . . fraction
friction . . . . friction
frustration . . . . frustration
fumigation . . . . fumigation
function . . . . fonction

generalization. . . . . généralisation
generation . . . . **génération**
germination . . . . germination
gestation . . . . gestation
globalization. . . . . globalisation
glorification . . . . glorification
gradation . . . . gradation
gravitation . . . . gravitation

habitation. . . . . habitation
hallucination . . . . hallucination
hesitation . . . . hésitation
hibernation . . . . hibernation
humiliation . . . . humiliation

identification . . . . identification
illumination . . . . illumination
illustration. . . . . illustration
imagination . . . . imagination
imitation . . . . **imitation**
"This painting is an imitation." . . **« Ce tableau est une imitation. »**
immigration . . . . immigration
immunization . . . . immunisation
imperfection . . . . imperfection
implication . . . . implication
importation . . . . importation
imposition. . . . . imposition
impregnation . . . . imprégnation
improvisation . . . . improvisation

inaction . . . . inaction
inauguration . . . . inauguration
incarceration. . . . . incarcération
incarnation . . . . incarnation
incineration. . . . . incinération
inclination. . . . . inclination
incrimination. . . . . incrimination
incubation . . . . incubation
indetermination . . . . indétermination
indication . . . . indication
indignation . . . . indignation
indiscretion . . . . indiscrétion *(meaning "nosiness," "inquisitiveness")*
infatuation . . . . infatuation *(meaning "vanity")*
infection . . . . infection *(also used for "stench," "vile smell")*
infiltration . . . . infiltration
inflammation. . . . . inflammation
inflation . . . . inflation
information . . . . **information**
inhibition . . . . inhibition
initiation . . . . initiation
injection . . . . injection
Inquisition. . . . . Inquisition
innovation . . . . innovation
inscription. . . . . inscription *(also used for "registration")*
insemination . . . . insémination
insertion . . . . insertion
inspection. . . . . inspection
inspiration . . . . inspiration *(also used for "breath," "inhalation")*
installation . . . . installation
institution . . . . institution
instruction. . . . . instruction
insurrection. . . . . insurrection
integration . . . . intégration

intensification . . . . intensification
intention . . . . **intention**
interaction . . . . interaction
interception. . . . . interception
interrogation . . . . interrogation
interruption . . . . interruption
interpretation . . . . interprétation
intersection . . . . intersection
intervention. . . . . intervention *(also used for "surgery," "operation")*
intimidation. . . . . intimidation
intonation . . . . intonation
intoxication. . . . . intoxication *(meaning "poisoning")*
introduction. . . . . introduction
introspection . . . . introspection
intuition . . . . intuition
inundation . . . . inondation
invention . . . . **invention**
investigation . . . . investigation
invitation . . . . invitation
irradiation . . . . irradiation
irrigation . . . . irrigation
irritation . . . . irritation
isolation . . . . isolation *(also used for "insulation")*

jubilation . . . . jubilation
jurisdiction . . . . juridiction
justification . . . . justification
juxtaposition . . . . juxtaposition

laceration . . . . lacération
lamentation. . . . . lamentation
legalization. . . . . légalisation
legislation. . . . . législation
levitation . . . . lévitation
liberation . . . . libération

limitation . . . . limitation
liquidation . . . . liquidation
locomotion . . . . locomotion
lotion . . . . **lotion**
lubrication . . . . lubrification

machination . . . . machination
malediction. . . . . malédiction
malformation. . . . . malformation
malnutrition. . . . . malnutrition
manifestation . . . . manifestation *(also used for "public demonstration")*
manipulation. . . . . manipulation
masturbation. . . . . masturbation
maturation . . . . maturation
maximization . . . . maximalisation
mechanization . . . . mécanisation
mediation. . . . . médiation
meditation . . . . méditation
mention . . . . mention *(noun only)*
migration . . . . migration
mobilization . . . . mobilisation
moderation. . . . . modération
modification . . . . modification
modulation. . . . . modulation
monopolization . . . . monopolisation
mortification . . . . mortification
motion . . . . motion *(only used for "proposal")*
motivation. . . . . motivation
multiplication . . . . multiplication
mutation. . . . . mutation
mutilation . . . . mutilation
mystification . . . . mystification

narration . . . . narration
nation . . . . **nation**

navigation . . . . navigation
negation. . . . . négation
negotiation . . . . négociation
nomination . . . . nomination
notation . . . . notation
notion . . . . notion
nutrition . . . . nutrition

objection . . . . objection
obligation. . . . . obligation
obliteration . . . . oblitération
observation. . . . . observation
obstruction . . . . obstruction
occupation . . . . occupation
operation . . . . **opération**
opposition . . . . opposition
option . . . . option
organization. . . . . organisation
orientation . . . . orientation
oxidation . . . . oxydation

pagination . . . . pagination
palpitation . . . . palpitation
participation . . . . participation
partition . . . . partition *(also used for "music score")*
penetration . . . . pénétration
perception . . . . perception
perdition . . . . perdition
perfection . . . . perfection
perforation . . . . perforation
permutation . . . . permutation
perpetuation . . . . perpétuation
persecution . . . . persécution
personification . . . . personnification
perspiration . . . . transpiration
petition. . . . . pétition

pigmentation . . . . pigmentation
plantation . . . . plantation
pollution . . . . pollution
popularization. . . . . popularisation
population . . . . **population**
portion . . . . portion
position . . . . **position** *(for employment, use "situation")*
potion . . . . potion
precaution . . . . précaution
precipitation . . . . précipitation
predestination . . . . prédestination
prediction . . . . prédiction
predilection. . . . . prédilection
predisposition . . . . prédisposition
premeditation . . . . préméditation
premonition . . . . prémonition
preoccupation . . . . **préoccupation**
"It's a constant preoccupation." . . . . **« C'est une préoccupation constante. »**
preparation. . . . . préparation
preposition . . . . préposition
presentation . . . . présentation
preservation . . . . préservation
presumption . . . . présomption
pretension. . . . . prétention
prevention . . . . prévention
privation. . . . . privation
privatization . . . . privatisation
probation . . . . probation
proclamation. . . . . proclamation
procreation. . . . . procréation
production . . . . production
prohibition . . . . prohibition
projection. . . . . projection
proliferation . . . . prolifération

prolongation . . . . prolongation
promotion. . . . . promotion
pronunciation . . . . pronunciation
proportion . . . . proportion
proposition . . . . proposition
prostitution . . . . prostitution
prostration . . . . prostration
protection . . . . protection
provocation . . . . provocation
publication . . . . publication
punctuation. . . . . ponctuation
purification . . . . purification
putrefaction . . . . putréfaction

qualification . . . . qualification
question . . . . question

radiation . . . . radiation
ramification . . . . ramification
ratification . . . . ratification
ration. . . . . ration
reaction . . . . **réaction**
"Your reaction is ridiculous." . . **« Ta réaction est ridicule. »**
realization . . . . réalisation *(meaning "completion")*
reception . . . . réception
recitation . . . . récitation
recommendation . . . . recommandation
reconciliation . . . . réconciliation
recreation. . . . . récréation
recrimination. . . . . récrimination
recuperation . . . . récupération
redemption . . . . rédemption
reduction . . . . réduction
reelection . . . . réélection
refraction . . . . réfraction
refrigeration . . . . réfrigération

reflection . . . . réflexion
regeneration . . . . régénération
regulation . . . . régulation
rehabilitation. . . . . réhabilitation
reincarnation . . . . réincarnation
relation . . . . relation
relegation . . . . relégation
remuneration. . . . . rémunération
renovation . . . . rénovation
renunciation . . . . renonciation
reorganization . . . . réorganisation
reparation . . . . réparation
repetition . . . . répétition
replication . . . . réplication
representation . . . . représentation
reproduction . . . . reproduction
reputation. . . . . **réputation**
"He has a bad reputation." . . **« Il a une mauvaise réputation. »**
requisition. . . . . réquisition
reservation . . . . réservation
resignation . . . . résignation *(only used for feelings; "job resignation" is "démission")*
resolution . . . . résolution
respiration . . . . respiration
restitution . . . . restitution
restoration . . . . restauration
restriction . . . . restriction
resurrection. . . . . résurrection
retention. . . . . rétention
retraction . . . . rétractation
retribution. . . . . rétribution
revelation . . . . révélation
reverberation . . . . réverbération
revocation . . . . révocation

revolution . . . . **révolution**

"There was a revolution.". . . . **« Il y a eu une révolution. »**

rotation . . . . rotation

salutation . . . . salutation

sanction . . . . sanction

satisfaction . . . . **satisfaction**

saturation . . . . saturation

secretion. . . . . sécrétion

section . . . . section

sedation . . . . sédation

sedition . . . . sédition

seduction . . . . séduction

sedimentation . . . . sédimentation

segmentation . . . . segmentation

segregation . . . . ségrégation

selection. . . . . sélection

self-destruction. . . . . autodestruction

sensation . . . . sensation

separation . . . . séparation

simplification. . . . . simplification

simulation. . . . . simulation

situation . . . . **situation** *(also used for "job position")*

"The situation is difficult.". . . . **« La situation est difficile. »**

solution . . . . **solution**

"I don't see a solution." . . . . . **« Je ne vois pas de solution. »**

specialization . . . . spécialisation

specification . . . . spécification

speculation . . . . spéculation

stabilization . . . . stabilisation

stagnation . . . . stagnation

station . . . . **station** *(only used for "bus station"; "train station" is "gare")*

"The bus station is close." . . . **« La station de bus est proche. »**

sterilization. . . . . stérilisation

stimulation . . . . stimulation

stipulation . . . . stipulation
strangulation . . . . strangulation
subordination . . . . subordination
substitution . . . . substitution
subtraction . . . . soustraction
suffocation . . . . suffocation
suggestion . . . . suggestion
superstition . . . . superstition
supposition . . . . supposition
synchronization . . . . synchronisation

taxation . . . . taxation *(more commonly "imposition")*
telecommunication . . . . télécommunication
temptation . . . . tentation
traction . . . . traction
tradition . . . . **tradition**
"It's a tradition." . . . . **« C'est une tradition. »**
transaction . . . . transaction
transcription . . . . transcription
transformation . . . . transformation
transition . . . . transition
translation . . . . traduction
trepidation . . . . trépidation
tribulation . . . . tribulations *(only used in the plural)*

unification . . . . unification
urbanization . . . . urbanisation
utilization . . . . utilisation

vaccination . . . . vaccination
validation . . . . validation
variation . . . . variation
vegetation . . . . végétation
veneration . . . . vénération
ventilation . . . . ventilation
verification . . . . vérification

vibration . . . . vibration
violation . . . . violation
vocation . . . . vocation
vocalization . . . . vocalisation

Reliez les paires de mots synonymes ou associés.

1. station	circonstance
2. situation	route
3. réaction	donation
4. direction	bus
5. célébration	anniversaire
6. contribution	pays
7. nation	réponse

22B.

Ecoutez et lisez l'histoire. Répondez aux questions suivantes avec des phrases complètes.

Dans la station de bus d'Orléans, Philippe et Marie voient une affiche (a sign) **pour une grande célébration sur la place principale ce soir. Ils lisent l'information et comprennent que ce sera une grande fête. Marie ne veut pas y aller parce qu'elle ne se sent pas bien** (she doesn't feel well)**. Philippe dit : « À ton tour de me faire une faveur. » Marie voit que la réaction de Philippe est forte et elle dit : « Très bien, allons-y. » Philippe dit : « Quelle grande célébration ! Ce sont des conditions parfaites pour découvrir cette belle ville et sa cuisine. » La réaction de Marie est plus sobre** (subdued)**. Elle dit : « Oui, nous avons une bonne position ici. » A la fin de la fête, Philippe est plus calme. Il dit : « Marie, j'ai trop mangé et trop bu, je dois aller dormir. »**

1. Où voient-ils l'affiche pour la célébration ?

2. Comment sera cette fête ?

3. Pourquoi est-ce que la célébration est intéressante pour Philippe ?

4. Comment est la réaction de Marie ?

5. À la fin de la fête comment se sent Philippe ?

Chapter 23

English words ending in "–ty" generally correspond to "–té" in French.

French words ending in "–té" are usually feminine nouns. For example,

an activity = *une activité*

All words and phrases in **bold** *are on* **Track 23** *of the accompanying audio.*

ENGLISH . . . . FRENCH

abnormality . . . . anormalité
absurdity . . . . absurdité
accessibility . . . . accessibilité
acidity . . . . acidité
activity . . . . **activité**
actuality . . . . actualité *(also used for "news," "current events")*
adversity . . . . adversité
affinity . . . . affinité
agility . . . . agilité
ambiguity . . . . ambiguïté
amenity . . . . aménité *(meaning "pleasantness")*
amorality . . . . amoralité
animosity . . . . animosité
antiquity . . . . antiquité *(also used for "antiques")*
anxiety . . . . **anxiété**
atrocity . . . . atrocité
austerity . . . . austérité
authenticity . . . . authenticité
authority . . . . autorité
avidity . . . . avidité

banality . . . . banalité

beauty . . . . beauté
bestiality. . . . . bestialité
brevity . . . . brièveté
brutality . . . . brutalité

calamity . . . . calamité
capacity . . . . capacité
captivity . . . . captivité
cavity. . . . . cavité *(for teeth, use "carrie")*
celebrity . . . . **célébrité**
charity . . . . charité
chastity. . . . . chasteté
city . . . . cité *(only used for "historic center" of a city)*
civility . . . . civilité
clarity. . . . . clarté
commodity . . . . commodité *(meaning "convenience," "comfort")*
community . . . . **communauté** *(only used in a cultural or religious context)*
compatibility . . . . compatibilité
complexity . . . . complexité
complicity. . . . . complicité
confidentiality . . . . confidentialité
conformity . . . . conformité
continuity . . . . continuité
cordiality . . . . cordialité
creativity . . . . **créativité**
"He has a lot of creativity." . . **« Il a beaucoup de créativité. »**
credibility . . . . crédibilité
credulity . . . . crédulité
cruelty . . . . cruauté
culpability. . . . . culpabilité
curiosity . . . . **curiosité**

debility. . . . . débilité

deformity . . . . difformité
density . . . . densité
deputy . . . . député *(meaning "elected official")*
dexterity . . . . dextérité
difficulty . . . . **difficulté**
dignity . . . . dignité
disparity . . . . disparité
diversity . . . . diversité
divinity . . . . divinité
duality . . . . dualité
duplicity . . . . duplicité
durability . . . . durabilité

eccentricity . . . . excentricité
elasticity . . . . élasticité
electricity . . . . **électricité**
enormity . . . . énormité
entity . . . . entité
equality . . . . égalité
equity . . . . équité
eternity . . . . éternité
eventuality . . . . éventualité
extremity . . . . extrémité

facility . . . . facilité *(meaning "ease" or "ability")*
faculty . . . . faculté *(meaning "ability" and "university department")*
falsity . . . . fausseté
familiarity . . . . familiarité
fatality . . . . fatalité *(meaning "fate")*
feasibility . . . . faisabilité
felicity . . . . félicité
femininity . . . . féminité
ferocity . . . . férocité
fertility . . . . fertilité

fidelity . . . . fidélité
flexibility . . . . **flexibilité**
"His flexibility is exceptional." . . . . **« Sa flexibilité est exceptionnelle. »**
fluidity . . . . fluidité
formality. . . . . formalité
fragility . . . . fragilité
fraternity. . . . . fraternité
frugality . . . . frugalité
futility. . . . . futilité

gaiety . . . . gaieté
generality. . . . . généralité
generosity . . . . **générosité**
gratuity . . . . gratuité *(meaning "free," "no cost")*
gravity . . . . gravité

heredity . . . . hérédité
hilarity . . . . hilarité
heterosexuality . . . . hétérosexualité
homosexuality. . . . . homosexualité
honesty . . . . honnêteté
hospitality. . . . . hospitalité
hostility. . . . . hostilité
humanity . . . . humanité
humidity . . . . humidité
humility . . . . humilité

identity. . . . . **identité**
"Here is my ID (identity) card.". . **« Voici ma carte d'identité. »**
illegality . . . . illégalité
immaturity. . . . . immaturité
immensity . . . . immensité
immobility. . . . . immobilité
immorality . . . . immoralité
immortality . . . . immortalité

immunity. . . . . immunité
impartiality . . . . impartialité
impetuosity . . . . impétuosité
impiety. . . . . impiété
impossibility . . . . **impossibilité**
improbability . . . . improbabilité
impunity . . . . impunité
impurity . . . . impureté
inactivity. . . . . inactivité
incapacity. . . . . incapacité
incompatibility. . . . . incompatibilité
incongruity . . . . incongruité
incredulity. . . . . incrédulité
indemnity . . . . indemnité
indignity. . . . . indignité
individuality . . . . individualité
indivisibility. . . . . indivisibilité
inequality . . . . inégalité
infallibility. . . . . infaillibilité
inferiority . . . . infériorité
infertility . . . . infertilité
infidelity . . . . infidélité
infinity . . . . infinité *(more commonly* "infini"*)*
infirmity . . . . infirmité
inflammability . . . . inflammabilité
inflexibility . . . . inflexibilité
ingenuity . . . . ingéniosité
inhumanity . . . . inhumanité
iniquity. . . . . iniquité
insatiability . . . . insatiabilité
insensibility. . . . . insensibilité
insensitivity . . . . insensibilité
instability . . . . instabilité
integrity . . . . intégrité
intensity . . . . **intensité**
invincibility . . . . invincibilité

invisibility . . . . invisibilité
irregularity . . . . irrégularité
irresponsibility. . . . . irresponsabilité

legality. . . . . légalité
liberty . . . . **liberté**
"I visited the Statue of Liberty." . . . . **« J'ai visité la statue de la Liberté. »**
liquidity . . . . liquidité
longevity . . . . longévité
loyalty . . . . loyauté
lucidity . . . . lucidité *(more commonly* "clarté"*)*

magnanimity. . . . . magnanimité
majesty . . . . majesté
majority . . . . majorité *(also used for "adulthood")*
masculinity . . . . masculinité
maternity . . . . maternité
maturity . . . . maturité
mediocrity . . . . médiocrité
mentality . . . . mentalité
minority . . . . minorité *(also used for "under 18 years old")*
mobility . . . . mobilité
modernity. . . . . modernité
monstrosity . . . . monstruosité
morality . . . . moralité
mortality. . . . . mortalité
multiplicity . . . . multiplicité
municipality . . . . municipalité

nationality . . . . nationalité
nativity. . . . . nativité
necessity. . . . . **nécessité**
neutrality . . . . neutralité
normality . . . . normalité

notoriety . . . . notoriété
novelty . . . . nouveauté
nudity. . . . . nudité

obesity . . . . obésité
objectivity. . . . . objectivité
obscenity . . . . obscénité
obscurity . . . . obscurité
opportunity. . . . . **opportunité** *(more commonly "occasion")*
originality. . . . . originalité

parity . . . . parité
partiality. . . . . partialité
particularity . . . . particularité
passivity. . . . . passivité
paternity. . . . . paternité
peculiarity . . . . particularité
penalty. . . . . pénalité
perpetuity . . . . perpétuité
perplexity . . . . perplexité
personality . . . . **personnalité**
"He has a charming personality." . . . . **« Il a une charmante personnalité. »**
perversity . . . . perversité
piety . . . . piété
placidity. . . . . placidité
plasticity. . . . . plasticité
plausibility . . . . plausibilité
plurality . . . . pluralité
polarity . . . . polarité
popularity. . . . . popularité
possibility . . . . **possibilité**
posterity . . . . postérité
poverty. . . . . pauvreté
principality . . . . principauté

priority . . . . priorité
probability . . . . probabilité
productivity. . . . . productivité
promiscuity . . . . promiscuité
property . . . . propriété
prosperity. . . . . prospérité
proximity . . . . proximité
puberty . . . . puberté
publicity . . . . publicité *(also used for "advertising")*
punctuality . . . . ponctualité
purity . . . . pureté

quality . . . . **qualité**
quantity . . . . **quantité**

rapidity . . . . rapidité
rarity . . . . rareté
rationality. . . . . rationalité
reality . . . . réalité
reciprocity . . . . réciprocité
regularity . . . . régularité
relativity . . . . relativité
respectability . . . . respectabilité
responsibility. . . . . **responsabilité**
"I have a lot of responsibilities." . . . . **« J'ai beaucoup de responsabilités. »**
rigidity . . . . rigidité
royalty . . . . royauté

sanctity. . . . . sainteté
satiety . . . . satiété
security. . . . . sécurité
senility . . . . sénilité
sensibility . . . . sensibilité *(also used for "sensitivity")*
sensuality . . . . sensualité
sentimentality . . . . sentimentalité

serenity . . . . sérénité
severity. . . . . sévérité
sexuality . . . . sexualité
similarity. . . . . similarité
simplicity . . . . simplicité
sincerity . . . . sincérité
singularity. . . . . singularité
sobriety . . . . sobriété
society . . . . société
solemnity . . . . solennité
solidarity . . . . solidarité
solidity . . . . solidité
solubility. . . . . solubilité
speciality . . . . **spécialité**
specificity . . . . spécificité
spirituality. . . . . spiritualité
spontaneity . . . . spontanéité
stability . . . . stabilité
sterility . . . . stérilité
stupidity . . . . stupidité
subjectivity . . . . subjectivité
subtlety. . . . . subtilité
superiority . . . . supériorité
surety . . . . sûreté *(also used for "safety," "sureness")*

tangibility . . . . tangibilité
technicality . . . . technicité
tenacity . . . . ténacité
timidity. . . . . timidité
tonality. . . . . tonalité
totality . . . . totalité
tranquility . . . . tranquillité
treaty . . . . traité *(also used for "treatise")*
trinity . . . . trinité
triviality . . . . trivialité *(also used for "vulgarity")*

ubiquity . . . . ubiquité
unanimity . . . . unanimité
uniformity . . . . uniformité
unity . . . . unité
university . . . . **université**
"You are going to the university." . . . . **« Tu vas à l'université. »**
utility . . . . utilité *(meaning "usefulness")*

validity . . . . validité
vanity . . . . vanité
variety . . . . variété
velocity . . . . vélocité
veracity . . . . véracité
verity . . . . vérité *(meaning "truth")*
versatility . . . . versatilité *(meaning "fickleness")*
viability . . . . viabilité
virginity . . . . virginité
virility . . . . virilité
virtuosity . . . . virtuosité
viscosity . . . . viscosité
visibility . . . . **visibilité**
vitality . . . . vitalité
vivacity . . . . vivacité
volatility . . . . volatilité
voracity . . . . voracité
vulgarity . . . . vulgarité
vulnerability . . . . vulnérabilité

23A.

Reliez les paires de mots synonymes ou associés.

1. université	chance
2. difficulté	abondance
3. impossibilité	imagination
4. activité	mouvement
5. opportunité	professeur
6. créativité	infaisabilité
7. quantité	obstacle

23B.

Ecoutez et lisez l'histoire. Répondez aux questions suivantes avec des phrases complètes.

La dernière ville (last city) **pour Philippe et Marie, c'est Versailles. Marie est très enthousiaste ; elle dit que Versailles est une ville où il y a beaucoup de créativité, d'originalité et d'activité. Philippe dit qu'il aime beaucoup la personnalité de cet endroit. Versailles est une belle ville et ils y restent quatre jours. Un jour Marie croit voir** (she thinks she sees) **une célébrité : Jean Reno. Mais Philippe dit que c'est impossible, parce que Jean Reno tourne un film en Suisse. Avant de rentrer à la maison** (before going home), **Philippe dit : « Écoute Marie, j'ai une question, est-ce que nous pourrions vivre ici, à Versailles, un jour ? » Marie répond : « Oui, oui, il y a beaucoup de possibilités pour nous ici. On va voir.... »**

1. Que dit Marie de Versailles ?

2. Qu'est-ce que Philippe aime dans cette ville ?

3. Combien de jours restent-ils à Versailles?

4. Est-ce que Marie voit une célébrité ?

5. Est-ce que Marie veut vivre à Versailles un jour ? Qu'est-ce qu'elle dit ?

ANSWER KEY

1A.

1. animal: zoo
2. total: complet
3. social: convivial
4. original: unique
5. légal: permis
6. crucial: essentiel
7. principal: capital

1B.

1. Ils sont de Strasbourg.
2. Il veut faire un voyage international.
3. Elle veut faire un voyage national.
4. Il dit que l'idée de Marie n'est pas originale.
5. Selon Philippe, l'oncle de Marie est trop antisocial et traditionnel.

2A.

1. distance: loin
2. ambulance: hôpital
3. tolérance: respect
4. arrogance: vanité
5. importance: proéminence
6. persévérance: détermination
7. fragrance: parfum

2B.

1. Il parle de l'importance de ne pas dépenser beaucoup.
2. Oui, il y a beaucoup de distance à parcourir.
3. Il faudra de la persévérance.
4. Oui, elle comprend l'importance de ne pas dépenser beaucoup d'argent.
5. Il répond : « On va voir.... »

3A.

1. restaurant: dîner
2. important: essentiel
3. élégant: chic
4. abondant: copieux
5. arrogant: vanité
6. immigrant: étranger
7. éléphant: animal

3B.

1. Ils vont à Paris.
2. Elle pense qu'ils sont arrogants.
3. Il dit que leur façon de s'habiller est élégante.
4. Il dit que l'histoire de Paris est très importante.
5. Le restaurant s'appelle L'éléphant rouge.

4A.

1. spectaculaire: sensationnel
2. polaire: froid
3. solaire: soleil
4. circulaire: sphérique
5. nucléaire: atomique
6. vulgaire: indécent
7. cardio-vasculaire: cœur

4B.

1. Ils font une promenade.
2. Il utilise un téléphone portable.
3. Son italien est spectaculaire.
4. Il étudie la physique nucléaire.
5. Les conversations de son ami sont plutôt circulaires.

5A.

1. nécessaire: obligatoire
2. ordinaire: commun
3. contraire: opposé
4. anniversaire: célébration
5. dictionnaire: définition
6. salaire: argent
7. secrétaire: assistant

5B.

1. L'itinéraire de Philippe et Marie à Paris est très compliqué.
2. Elle filme un documentaire.
3. Il dit que le rythme est extraordinaire.
4. Selon Philippe, il n'est pas nécessaire de filmer chaque détail.
5. Elle répond : « Au contraire, c'est très important de filmer chaque détail ! »

6A.

1. visible: perceptible
2. incroyable: extraordinaire
3. horrible: très mal
4. inflexible: rigide
5. comparable: similaire
6. probable: possible
7. adorable: mignon

6B.

1. Après Paris, ils vont en Corse.
2. Elle pense que Philippe est très irresponsable.
3. Il dit que Marie est inflexible.
4. Non, elle pense que c'est assez improbable.
5. Elle demande s'il sera possible d'acheter les billets pour le spectacle de danse en Corse.

7A.

1. respect: admiration
2. direct: immédiat
3. correct: exact
4. contact: adresse
5. aspect: partie
6. exact: précis
7. incorrect: erroné

7B.

1. Ils ont pris un vol direct.
2. Elle pense que ce n'est pas la destination correcte parce qu'elle ne comprend pas tout.
3. Elle ne comprend pas le français en Corse parce qu'ils parlent un dialecte.
4. Le contact de Philippe s'appelle Alphonse.
5. Il a beaucoup de respect pour Philippe et sa petite amie Marie.

8A.

1. patience: calme
2. différence: distinction
3. innocence: naïveté
4. violence: guerre
5. science: biologie
6. conférence: réunion
7. expérience: maturité

8B.

1. Il dit : « Quelle coïncidence ! Ma petite amie et moi allons à la danse demain soir. »
2. Selon Marie, la persistance et la patience aident.
3. Il pense que ce sera une bonne expérience.
4. Il ressent de l'indifférence.
5. Il est désolé de son impatience.

9A.

1. président: directeur
2. urgent: pressant
3. continent: Europe
4. client: consommateur
5. patient: calme
6. intelligent: intellectuel
7. différent: distinct

9B.

1. Elle reçoit un message urgent.
2. Il est directeur d'un établissement médical.
3. Elle dit que son cousin est différent/compétent/intelligent/étrange.
4. Oui, selon Marie il est très, très intelligent.
5. Il dit : « Bon, on va voir.... »

10A.

1. allergie: pollen
2. stratégie: tactique
3. psychologie: mental
4. géologie: pierre
5. énergie: dynamisme
6. chronologie: temps
7. trilogie: trois

10B.

1. Il a beaucoup d'énergie.
2. Non, le café ne donne pas d'allergies aux jeunes.
3. Il parle de ses nouvelles technologies médicales.
4. Non, il n'étudie pas la radiologie.
5. Non, elle n'étudie pas la psychologie.

11A.

1. stratégique: tactique
2. électronique: radio
3. artistique: créatif
4. classique: romain
5. ironique: sarcastique
6. authentique: véritable
7. historique: date

11B.

1. Ils visitent des musées artistiques.
2. Nice est magique le soir.
3. Nice est une ville fantastique.
4. Quand il conduit, il y a beaucoup de circulation.
5. Selon Marie, ce n'est pas très romantique de passer les vacances en voiture.

12A.

1. typique: normal
2. botanique: jardin
3. pratique: rationnel
4. électrique: lampe
5. éthique: moralité
6. biologique: humain
7. magique: mystique

12B.

1. Il veut rester à Nice.
2. Elle veut voyager d'une façon logique.
3. Oui, elle a le sens pratique.
4. Ils vont à Marseille.
5. Elle dit : « Toi aussi tu veux aller à Marseille, pas vrai ? »

13A.

1. valide: vrai
2. rigide: inflexible
3. acide: citron
4. liquide: fluide
5. timide: réservé
6. stupide: idiot
7. splendide: magnifique

13B.

1. Elle dit que c'est un plan stupide.
2. Il pense que c'est une idée splendide.
3. Pendant le voyage il fait très humide.
4. Il dit qu'il doit boire beaucoup de liquide.
5. Il dit qu'il ne doit pas manger de nourriture acide.

14A.

1. communisme: Karl Marx
2. optimisme: positif
3. impressionisme: art
4. féminisme: femme
5. nationalisme: patriotisme
6. tourisme: passeport
7. terrorisme: bombe

14B.

1. Oui, il y a beaucoup de tourisme à Marseille.
2. Le livre parle de l'influence du socialisme, du fascisme et du communisme en France.
3. Le livre décrit le nationalisme français.
4. Elle demande à Philippe ce qu'il pense du capitalisme.
5. Il dit : « Mangeons une glace ! »

15A.

1. artiste: peintre
2. touriste: visiteur
3. pessimiste: négatif
4. optimiste: positif
5. dentiste: dent
6. finaliste: compétition
7. fleuriste: bouquet

15B.

1. Il est dentiste.
2. Oui, ce sont des touristes « professionnels. »
3. Elle a une liste de questions.
4. Le dentiste est pessimiste et réaliste.
5. L'artiste est optimiste et idéaliste.

16A.

1. consécutif: successif
2. créatif: artistique
3. positif: optimiste
4. exécutif: patron
5. motif: cause
6. négatif: fataliste
7. objectif: impartial

16B.

1. Il avait entendu des choses négatives.
2. Il pense que c'est une région créative et compétitive.
3. Elle a une impression positive.
4. Juvignac est un village pas très actif mais très accueillant.
5. Ils passent deux jours consécutifs là-bas.

17A.

1. docteur: médecin
2. acteur: théâtre
3. sénateur: congrès
4. professeur: université
5. inventeur: innovateur
6. moteur: voiture
7. terreur: peur

17B.

1. Elle remarque de la terreur.
2. Il dit : « Quelle erreur de venir ici ! »
3. Il dit : « Fais-moi une faveur : dis-moi que je n'ai pas besoin d'aller à cette fête. »
4. Non, l'acteur n'est pas célèbre.
5. Non, le sénateur est vieux.

18A.

1. territoire: zone
2. accessoire: ceinture
3. contradictoire: paradoxal
4. laboratoire: recherche
5. obligatoire: nécessaire
6. ivoire: éléphant
7. victoire: gagner

18B.

1. Il vont à Bordeaux.
2. Il aurait préféré une auberge.
3. Il dit que la fête était pire que le purgatoire.
4. Non, ce n'est pas vrai. Sa présence était obligatoire.
5. Non, il ne répond pas au dernier commentaire contradictoire de Marie.

19A.

1. spacieux: vaste
2. ambitieux: déterminé
3. curieux: inquisiteur
4. délicieux: appétissant
5. prestigieux: fameux
6. nerveux: émotionnel
7. généreux: charitable

19B.

1. La visite de Toulouse a été désastreuse.
2. Ils sont délicieux.
3. Il a dit qu'il y a un air mystérieux là-bas.
4. Le programme prestigieux est le programme de langues étrangères.
5. Leur hôtel est très spacieux.

20A.

1. mission: objectif
2. confusion: chaos
3. collision: impact
4. tension: anxiété
5. télévision: film
6. précision: exactitude
7. explosion: bombe

20B.

1. Sa mission est de trouver une nouvelle assiette en porcelaine.
2. Elle veut cette chose pour sa collection.
3. Elle dit : « Ma décision finale est prise ! »
4. Il a l'impression que Marie ne plaisante pas.
5. Il y avait un peu de confusion avec toutes les rues et les impasses.

21A.

1. métamorphose: changement
2. analyse: étude
3. crise: problème
4. emphase: accentuation
5. hypothèse: présomption
6. dialyse: sang
7. hypnose: pendule

21B.

1. Ils ne mettent pas vraiment l'accent sur la ballade touristique parce qu'ils connaissent déjà Tours assez bien.
2. Ils vont chercher un cousin de Philippe qui étudie à Tours.
3. Il écrit sa thèse sur la crise financière du tiers-monde
4. Non, il n'a pas d'hypothèse pour sa thèse.
5. Il demande : « Est-ce que tu peux m'aider ? »

22A.

1. station: bus
2. situation: circonstance
3. réaction: réponse
4. direction: route
5. célébration: anniversaire
6. contribution: donation
7. nation: pays

22B.

1. Ils voient l'affiche pour la célébration dans la station de bus.
2. Ce sera une grande fête.
3. La célébration est intéressante pour Philippe parce qu'il veut découvrir cette belle ville et sa cuisine.
4. Sa réaction est plus sobre.
5. Il se sent plus calme.

23A.

1. université: professeur
2. difficulté: obstacle
3. impossibilité: infaisabilité
4. activité: mouvement
5. opportunité: chance
6. créativité: imagination
7. quantité: abondance

23B.

1. Elle dit que Versailles est une ville où il y a beaucoup de créativité, d'originalité et d'activité.
2. Il aime beaucoup la personnalité de cette ville.
3. Ils restent quatre jours à Versailles.
4. Non, elle croit voir une célébrité.
5. Oui, elle veut vivre à Versailles un jour. Elle dit : « Il y a beaucoup de possibilités pour nous ici. »

Audio files available for download at
Hippocrenebooks.com

AUDIO TRACK LIST

	English suffix	French suffix
Track 1 (3:57)	–al	–al
Track 2 (1:53)	–ance	–ance
Track 3 (2:36)	–ant	–ant
Track 4 (2:06)	–ar	–aire
Track 5 (2:29)	–ary	–arie
Track 6 (3:45)	–ble	–ble
Track 7 (1:57)	–ct	–ct
Track 8 (2:54)	–ence	–ence
Track 9 (2:49)	–ent	–ent
Track 10 (2:38)	–gy	–gie
Track 11 (4:01)	–ic	–ique
Track 12 (2:16)	–ical	–ique
Track 13 (1:53)	–id	–ide
Track 14 (2:53)	–ism	–isme
Track 15 (2:54)	–ist	–iste
Track 16 (3:00)	–ive	–if (–ive)
Track 17 (3:24)	–or	–eur
Track 18 (1:40)	–ory	–orie
Track 19 (2:51)	–ous	–eux (–euse)
Track 20 (2:49)	–sion	–sion
Track 21 (2:00)	–sis	–se
Track 22 (4:50)	–tion	–tion
Track 23 (2:54)	–ty	–té
Track 24 (2:54)	Pronunciation Guide	

www.ingramcontent.com/pod-product-compliance
Lightning Source LLC
Chambersburg PA
CBHW061301110426
42742CB00012BA/2008

9780781814485